ORGANIZATION AND ADMINISTRATION OF SERVICE PROGRAMS FOR THE OLDER AMERICAN

RICHARD E. HARDY, Ed.D.
Diplomate in Counseling Psychology

JOHN G. CULL, Ph.D.

CHARLES C THOMAS • PUBLISHER
Springfield • Illinois • U.S.A.

Published and Distributed Throughout the World by
CHARLES C THOMAS • PUBLISHER
Bannerstone House
301-327 East Lawrence Avenue, Springfield, Illinois, U.S.A.

© *1975, by* CHARLES C THOMAS • THOMAS

ISBN 0-398-03286-6

Library of Congress Catalog Card Number: 74-33807

Printed in the United States of America
R-1

Library of Congress Cataloging in Publication Data

Hardy, Richard E.   co-author Cull, John G.

Organization and administration of service programs
for the older Americans
74-33807
ISBN 0-398-03286-6

ORGANIZATION AND ADMINISTRATION OF SERVICE PROGRAMS FOR THE OLDER AMERICAN

Publication No. 968

AMERICAN LECTURE SERIES®

A Publication in

The BANNERSTONE DIVISION *of* AMERICAN LECTURES
IN SOCIAL AND REHABILITATION PSYCHOLOGY

Editors of the Series

JOHN G. CULL, Ph.D.

Director, Regional Counselor Training Program
Department of Rehabilitation Counseling
Virginia Commonwealth University
Fishersville, Virginia

RICHARD E. HARDY, Ed.D.

Diplomate in Counseling Psychology, ABPP
Chairman, Department of Rehabilitation Counseling
Virginia Commonwealth University
Richmond, Virginia

The American Lecture Series in Social and Rehabilitation Psychology offers books which are concerned with man's role in his milieu. Emphasis is placed on how this role can be made more effective in a time of social conflict and a deteriorating physical environment. The books are oriented toward descriptions of what future roles should be and are not concerned exclusively with the delineation and definition of contemporary behavior. Contributors are concerned to a considerable extent with prediction through the use of a functional view of man as opposed to a descriptive, anatomical point of view.

Books in this series are written mainly for the professional practitioner; however, academicians will find them of considerable value in both undergraduate and graduate courses in the helping services.

CONTRIBUTORS

Administration on Aging

Jane F. Connolly

John G. Cull

John T. Gardiner

Richard E. Hardy

Hawaii, County of, Senior Citizens Program

Health, Education and Welfare (HEW), Department of, and Staff

Sue Hecht

Delphine Lucero

Marjorie W. Lundy

Doris Anne Miller

Ruby L. Schmidt

Elmer H. Shafer

Patricia L. Sharpe

James L. Stewart

Anne R. Sullivan

Joseph G. Zieber

PREFACE

THE development of this book has been a long and tedious process. We are greatly indebted to many contributors who have provided materials describing their programs. We also appreciate the opportunity to get to know so many of them well and to work closely with them.

We have tried to carefully describe a representative example of various service programs for the older American throughout the United States. These programs vary widely in scope, purpose, goal and achievements.

During the last two decades our aging population has steadily grown in size. The contemporary older American developed during the period of time in which our culture readily accepted the dicta and pronouncements of authority figures. Our older citizens have been inculcated with the concept that there is an inherent justice in society — you get what you deserve — all comes to he who waits. Contemporary values have changed radically. We live in an era of mass demonstrations, violence, and transportation and social problems. We have become youth oriented as a result of the stronger demands of youth. Older persons are now the lost generation — a generation whose day did not arrive. The role their elders played in the culture and the role they expected to mature into has become nonfunctional in many cases. There has been a breakdown of the social values, customs and mores which many have held so dear. This segment of our population is angered, bewildered, concerned, and groping for a meaningful place in society.

This text is an attempt in describing services available to these persons through service facilities for them. It is hoped that the information provided will be of value to all professionals concerned with services to the older American and to older Americans themselves who are seeking out various types of social and rehabilitation services available to them.

RICHARD E. HARDY
JOHN G. CULL

Richmond, Virginia

CONTENTS

ORGANIZATION AND ADMINISTRATION OF SERVICE PROGRAMS FOR THE OLDER AMERICAN

CHAPTER 1

AGING SERVICE PROGRAMS TO END ISOLATION*

A MIX OF OPTIONS
TRANSPORTATION FOR OLDER PEOPLE
SENIOR CENTERS
GOOD NUTRITION FOR OLDER PEOPLE
TELEPHONE REASSURANCE
FRIENDLY VISITING
IN-HOME SERVICES FOR OLDER PEOPLE
OPPORTUNITIES TO SERVE
OUTREACH SERVICES
INFORMATION AND REFERRAL SERVICES

FIVE million older Americans live alone.

Many of them are active, well, and continue to take part in community life. But hundreds of thousands of them — even those who are mobile and could participate — live in virtual isolation. The phone does not ring, there are no visitors, there are no invitations, there are no easy, affordable ways to secure transportation to a senior center, a civic program, or even to market. There are no incentives to action.

And for the frailest, the truly physically homexound, life is lived in a kind of solitary confinement destructive to mental and physical health and to humanity.

We have the tools to combat this dreadful isolation for older people. Programs to do this exist, at least in part, or could be created, in every community.

Transportation, specially adapted to the physical needs of older people, to their timetables, to the routes that will take them where they need and wish to go, at a cost they can

*Let's End Isolation, DHEW Publication No. (SRS) 73-20129.

afford in spite of lowered incomes.

. Senior centers which reach out with real services, as well as recreation, to bring people into the action center of a community's life.

. Nutrition programs, which provide meals for older people in social settings, so that they may gain friendship, social contacts, education, and activity, as well as improvement in health through proper nutrition.

. Opportunities in paid employment and in volunteer activities to serve others — chances to be needed — the most necessary of human requirements.

. Home services to make independent living more possible.

All of these separate services need a slightly new focus. They need to be expanded, to have gaps filled, to be interrelated — transportation and places to go — in an all-out attack on isolation. It will, of course, require money but, more important, a tremendous commitment of thought, sensitivity, attention, and planning.

The result in human happiness and dignity will be worth it.

A MIX OF OPTIONS

Older people are not all isolated for the same reasons and they do not all need the same services.

This chapter reports upon a number of special community services, each designed to relieve isolation of older people in some way and to some degree.

Often one service in itself is useless without a companion service. Many excellent health or recreational programs, for example, are not fully used by older persons because they lack transportation to reach them. Sometimes an older person not only needs transportation to a welfare department office or a health clinic, but also needs someone to accompany him and stay with him, to see that he gets the service he is entitled to, and to see that he understands what is being done.

An older woman, referred to an excellent hospital clinic because she had glaucoma, received good medical care but little reassurance. In the busy clinic, she either did not ask her doctor or did not understand his answers. When visited at home by a volunteer, she asked, "Am I going to die?" She needed someone to explain glaucoma to her in simple terms, and to reassure her that while it was a serious condition it was not a life or death illness.

Some services serve more than one purpose at the same time. Telephone reassurance helps insure safety and also provides a personal contact, a kind of friendly vocal visiting. Some telephone reassurance services provide an information and referral component.

Congregate dining programs — nutritious meals in group settings — promote friendship as well as good health. These dining programs often actively seek out and invite isolated older persons to take part. They also may provide transportation to the dining room and serve as catalysts for formation of senior clubs.

TRANSPORTATION FOR OLDER PEOPLE

Lack of means to move around a community can isolate a healthy and physically mobile person as completely as if she were bedridden. Most older people don't drive. Taxis are too expensive for many of them. Public transportation either does not exist or is extremely difficult for them to use. It, too, grows more expensive every day.

As a result, many older people do not use available free medical services or facilities because they cannot reach them. They can't enjoy free concerts or visits to the park for the same reason.

Small neighborhood shops, easy to reach on foot, have disappeared in many communities. Today's supermarkets are often located at distances too great for many older people to reach by walking, particularly with heavy packages to carry home. And so nutrition suffers.

Financial problems may reach an unnecessary crisis when people have no way to get to a social security or public assistance office.

Some older people need an escort on trips either because of physical frailty or, in some areas, because they are afraid — with reason — to venture out alone.

Part-time jobs and volunteer opportunities, which would keep many people active, are prohibitively expensive because of high transportation fares.

A number of means for meeting these problems of mobility have developed in communities across the country.

Special Bus or Van

Some community and voluntary organizations sponsor a special bus or van to take older people on needed trips.

In Chicago, the YMCA with Administration on Aging (AoA) demonstration grant support, set up the Senior Citizens Mobile Service. In a 3-year demonstration, the Mobile Service provided transportation to 1,606 different seniors on a total of 30,403 trips. Forty-eight different agencies participated through referrals and requests for service.

Appointments for trips were scheduled a day ahead, and the central office was able to communicate with the van driver by two-way radio, allowing last-minute changes and emergencies to be handled.

Many persons have said that they feel 10 to 15 years younger as a result of the service. Some were able to go beyond their immediate neighborhoods for the first time in their lives. Many made enduring friendships during their rides together.

Although the demonstration grant funds for this project have ended, the Mobile Service is continuing operation with local funding. The Martin Luther King Urban Progress Center was impressed enough to give $20,000 toward the project's continuation.

South Providence, R.I., once a thriving section with grocery stores, banks, and doctor's offices in every block or two, has lost many of its stores, banks and doctors in recent years. To help approximately 2,000 older persons still living there to do their shopping and reach services in other parts of town, a station wagon was purchased by the Rhode Island Division on Aging. It averages 12 calls a day. Most trips are to doctor's offices, clinics and hospitals, but many people use this service to go grocery shopping. One trip usually serves several people at a time.

Texas "Roadrunner" Volunteers, Inc., a group in Austin,

Texas, which calls upon nursing home residents — leased a station wagon and a small bus primarily to take the patients on needed trips. When it was found that many former volunteer-visitors had dropped out of the program because they no longer felt able to drive their own cars, "Roadrunners" provided *their* transportation and they were again able to donate their services to the community.

In nine Missouri counties a variety of U.S. Government surplus vehicles serve the transportation needs of all ages including older people. Some vehicles are available on call; others run a regular route. Operating costs of the system are built into the budget of the Community Action Agency (OEO). Paid staff members and volunteers, including senior citizens, run the service. The Welfare Department pays for persons on public assistance. Riders in better financial circumstances who use the service sometimes make financial contributions. The CAA is presently considering converting this service into a transportation cooperative owned and operated by an incorporated membership group of rider-consumers.

Senior Center Bus Services

Some senior centers provide a bus that runs between the members' homes and the centers.

In Prince Georges County, Maryland, a sprawling suburban area, buses make stops at designated points to pick up groups of senior center members. The same buses sometimes take members on tours or sightseeing trips away from the centers.

"Dial-a-Bus" is a system operated by Little House Senior Center in Menlo Park, California. Center members may have a standing reservation, or they may phone in by noon of the day they wish to ride. A 12-passenger bus is driven along three regular routes by Little House members. In addition to regular runs, the bus is used for group outings and regular visits to four convalescent homes in the area where Little House members entertain the residents.

There is no charge for this bus service but Little House estimates it costs 60 cents a person per ride. This includes gas, insurance, and amortization of the vehicle. Many members contribute funds for the minibus operation.

Private Cars

Volunteers driving private cars have given older citizens of South Routt County, Colorado a choice of services and opportunities which were closed to them for lack of public transportation. In this high country, with low temperatures and lots of snow, even a few miles is a very long distance. No accessible public transportation exists.

Because a number of the small communities lack medical services, many of the trips are to doctor's offices. Other trips take senior citizens to polling places. In one instance, after almost a lifetime of residence in this country, three volunteer rides to Denver made it possible for an elderly woman to receive her U.S. citizenship. With it, she was able to qualify for Medicare!

Funded by the Colorado State Agency on Aging, with local sponsorship by the Visiting Nurse Association, this project is opening many additional opportunities for older citizens as their communities become more aware of them and their needs.

In four counties of Pennsylvania, STRIDE (Small Transportation Required in Developing Economy) serves the need of all age groups including the elderly. It too, uses privately-owned vehicles.

These vehicles, however, are not necessarily driven by their owners. Some persons drive their own cars to work in the morning and instead of parking them where they would be idle, turn them over to STRIDE drivers. The cars are returned to their owners at the end of the workday. Funded by the Office of Economic Opportunity, STRIDE has a board of directors and neighborhood councils in each community.

Reduced Fares

At least 50 cities with public transportation systems have experimented with reducing fares for older people during non-rush hours.

New York City and Chicago charge half-fare; San Francisco charges five cents a ride; Seattle and Tacoma, Washington, charge two dollars for a monthly pass which can be used during non-rush hours.

In several instances, reduced fares have not only made life happier for older citizens, but have increased ridership to the point of increasing transit companies' total revenues.

The small town of Commerce, California, provides free bus service to people of all ages within its city limits and to a major shopping center outside the city. Buses run every half-hour. No one has more than a block to walk from any point in the 8-square mile community to a bus stop.

Any organization with its membership composed of at least 60 percent Commerce city residents may schedule two free chartered bus trips per year to any destination within 50 miles of the city. Organizations, including three senior citizens organizations, use the free bus to go to ball games, museums, plays and other events. Commerce, a suburb of Los Angeles, has a population of 10,000 people. Total cost of the 5-bus system is $100,000 per year.

Physical Barriers

For some people, physical barriers in public transportation systems discourage use. These barriers include high bus steps, lurching vehicles, unsheltered bus stops, fast-moving escalators and turnstiles in subway stations. All can be overcome by thoughtfulness in the design of original equipment or replacement equipment.

Buses, for example, can be built so that their doors open at curb level by placing engine equipment on top of the bus instead of under it; automatic devices similar to those which collect road tolls could replace inconvenient subway turnstiles; one-way doors to control traffic, and gradual acceleration and deceleration to prevent jolting, are other feasible improvements which could be made in public transportation.

SENIOR CENTERS

Senior Centers are places where older person can come together for a variety of activities and programs. These range from just sitting and talking or playing cards, to professionally-directed hobby and group activities. Some centers provide counseling services to help individuals make better use of personal and community resources. Some assume responsibility for encouraging other community agencies to provide more help to senior citizens. A few centers serve as central umbrella agencies for all activities and services relating to older people. They serve too, as recruiting spots for volunteers, offering opportunties to older people to serve others less active.

Some people believe that, in time, the senior center may come to hold a place in the older person's life equivalent to the central role now played by the school in the lives of the children.

An Administration on Aging project to develop a directory of senior centers in the United States in 1969, found more than 1,200 centers. To be counted in this survey, a center had to provide programs for older people at least 3 days a week.

Wide Variety

A senior center with a most comprehensive program is the Knowles Center in Nashville, Tennessee. Built in 1966, it has 12 satellite centers. It offers 60-cent luncheons 5 days a week, regular health education programs such as classes for diabetics and people with auditory loss, small group physical education, and paramedical services including glaucoma screenings and immunizations. A public health nurse is always available to members.

The Center has rooms for recreation and social activity, a library, and an auditorium. Frequent outdoor programs and trips are scheduled.

North Dakota senior centers by contrast, report individually modest programs. But there are centers in 77 communities using whatever local facilities are available. Each program is built around and tailored to the interest and needs of local senior citizens. One center features a weekly 25-cent luncheon.

Many centers have made significant improvements in their communities. After the Senior Center at Almont, population 160, built a park with lighting, benches, shelters, and horseshoe courts, the town paved a main street, installed running water, and is now building public housing, the first construction in the town in 80 years. In all, more than 9,000 older North Dakotans participate in these centers.

Hodson Center in New York City was the first publicity sponsored senior day center in the country. It began in 1943 as a direct result of the concern of Department of Welfare social investigators for the retired and lonely men and women they met. Its first site was a shed 30-by-80 feet, which had formerly been used as a Works Progress Administration depot for the distribution of clothing. Welfare Department employees cleaned and painted the shed, sewed curtains, "begged and borrowed" furniture. The present Hodson Center is located in a public housing project in space especially designed for day center operation.

The City of New York now has over 100 senior centers, sponsored by the city, religious organizations, unions, and other private, non-profit organizations.

Little House in Menlo Park, California, one of the first senior centers established under private sponsorship, began in 1949. Open seven days a week, busy Little House offers a complete range of activities for its members. Some of its rooms, including the kitchen, may be used by Little House members for private parties. Peninsula Volunteers the founding organization continues to operate Little House and also sponsors housing and transportation for seniors.

Location is Important

Accessibility to older people is one of the main criteria for selecting a senior center location. Many kinds of buildings have been used. In Florence, Colorado, a former railroad station was converted into a center. In many public housing projects, space is provided for centers, open to the neighborhood residents as well as to those living in the project.

Many centers are built or rehabilitated by seniors themselves. In Spanish Fork, Utah, an $80,000 structure was built with an appropriation of $25,000 from the city council plus the volunteer labor of scores of craftsmen of all ages, and donations of cash and supplies.

Although most centers have a minimum age limit for members, in Plymouth, Wisconsin (population 5,200) seniors welcome younger adults to take part in programs. It is not unusual to see a mother and daughter in a sketching class together, or a father and son playing cards with other members. The seniors feel this hospitality to other age groups helps everyone.

Many centers have educational classes as part of their total program. For example, St. Luke's School of Continuing Education in Oklahoma City which began as a church senior center, provides daily classes with a 75-cent meal available at lunchtime on Fridays. Courses include Spanish, archaeology, creative writing, piano, painting, and whatever else the seniors request.

Tuition is $2 a semester and enrollment 1965 was over 700. For many people who have not had the educational opportunities of today's youth, the school is a dream come true.

GOOD NUTRITION FOR OLDER PEOPLE

Poor nutrition can be caused in part by isolation and loneliness which make it seem hardly worthwhile preparing food to eat alone.

Good nutrition, however, provided in a group setting, can offer a partial solution to loneliness. Throughout much of life, eating is a social occasion, a time for family gatherings and meetings with friends. Birthday parties, holidays, picnics — all are associated with pleasant times and food. When the social element is removed entirely, many people abandon regular mealtimes and turn to sporadic snacks to satisfy their hunger.

Group Meals

The benefit of eating is a social setting is so important for the mental as well as physical well-being of older people, regardless of income, that many organizations are providing group meals in a variety of settings.

Older people themselves, as volunteers, paid employees, or advisors, are important in the operation of these programs.

A location easily accessible to older people is the most important factor in choosing a serving-site, and actual meal preparation can often be handled in a location other than that where the food is to be served.

School cafeterias are frequently used to prepare food to be served in other locations, or in cafeterias after the students' lunch hour. The State of Massachusetts has passed legislation enabling any school cafeteria or other non-profit institution to serve lunches at a cost of 50 cents to persons over 59 years of age. The State reimburses the institutions for their expenses above 50 cents. There is no "means test" for older persons and some communities are able to meet their costs with the 50-cent charge needing no State subsidy.

In St. Louis, prepared food is delivered to neighborhood homes. Eight to 12 neighborhood residents meet at each home for a noon meal. In this way, food preparation is economical, meets all health department standards, and older people can get together informally and eat family style in small groups with a minimum of travel time or distance to cover.

SAMS (Serve-A-Meal to Seniors) serves meals to an average of 700 older people each week in five different locations in Denver, Colorado. Rent and utilities are paid by the five host organizations — three churches, a Salvation Army center, and the Urban Renewal Agency. The entree is prepared on site in small kitchens. Forty-five senior citizens are employed part-time by SAMS as ticket-sellers, custodians, hostesses. They administer the questionnaires used in the research phase of the project. Participants pay 60 cents for each meal.

Many group meal projects include programs featuring speakers on nutrition, health, social security and other topics of interest to older persons. Some senior clubs hold meetings in conjunction with a meal; others provide table games, entertainment, and time to "visit" before or after the meals.

In a number of AoA nutrition projects, occasional "pot luck" luncheons are prepared by participants. With careful planning on the part of the nutritionist of the project, these luncheons can become a very effective teaching tool. Participants prepare indivdual dishes in their own homes and bring them into the group setting in their own serving dishes. Preparation beforehand has included information on the value of a variety of good foods and the desirability of combining meat, vegetable, and fruit dishes in one meal. Lessons learned enjoyably on these occasions often carry over into continuing home nutrition habits.

The Detroit program has been including pot luck meals in its program for some months, and Helena, Montana, is just beginning them as one of several means of continuing of program.

Just as reduced fares for seniors are increasing ridership, some commercial restaurants and cafeterias are finding it profitable to serve well-balanced meals to older people at reduced prices. A Florida cafeteria chain is serving senior meals at 88 cents twice a day 7 days a week at four locations. A Los Angeles cafeteria chain offers special senior meals for $1 in nine locations 7 days a week between 1:30 and 4:30 p.m. A San Francisco restaurant offers a take-out package of breakfast, sandwich lunch, and a hot dinner for $2.

The fringe benefits of eating in a group are so great that professionals who work with older people urge that every effort be made to include handicapped elderly persons, even if they are blind, severely disabled, or in wheelchairs. Although some help must be given them, it makes the meal a social occasion for them and gives more active participants a chance to serve others.

The value of group meals within an institutional setting is reported in *Nursing Homes Magazine's* special food issue of February 1971. A series of weekly luncheons are held in a particular nursing home under the supervision of the home's activity leader, with individual invitations issued to two, three, or four patients. They are invited "to go out to lunch" — out of their nursing home room, that is, to a group meal in another part of the home. Gay tablecloths, flowers on the table, and menus are provided.

Results reported include new interest in life, new friendships even among those "who live on different floors," and deep appreciation from the patients. It takes about 6 months to go through the entire nursing home roster.

Meals-on-Wheels

Prepared hot meals, delivered to older persons' houses are popularly known as Meals-on-Wheels. They often consist of a hot noon meal and a cold supper left for evening use. In some communities, these meals are delivered by private automobiles; in others, special vehicles with equipment to keep food hot and cold are used.

Such home-delivered meals provide a daily link for the homebound with the outside world, someone to greet each day. Sometimes the volunteer stays to visit during the meal. Charges for this home delivery service vary, according to the organization sponsoring the program (volunteer or commercial), and according to the ability of the older person to pay. Inability to market, inability to prepare food and not having anyone to help on a regular basis are reasons this service is needed.

One of the largest home-delivered meal programs, Baltimore's Meals-on-Wheels, is run almost entirely by volunteers. It was begun in 1960 by the Baltimore Section of the National Council of Jewish Women with the guidance of the Maryland Home Economics Association. Other church groups joined and AoA funded a full time coordinator who is housed in the Lutheran Social Service Agency. Today Baltimore's Meals-on-Wheels program operates from nine separate kitchens — all but one located in churches. There is one paid coordinator and city, county and state nutritionists freely give help in planning menus.

The program charges ten dollars a week for those able to pay and delivers two meals daily, one hot, one cold, five days a week.

All meal recipients are given the phone number of the central intake office when they enter the programs. They may call to comment or complain about meals or service, or just to talk. If a person needs help other than food service, he is referred to an appropriate agency. Volunteers who deliver meals also may report a client's other needs which are followed up by the central office.

TELEPHONE REASSURANCE

Many older people who live alone fear that they may have a fall or be taken suddenly ill and be unable to call for help.

The first telephone reassurance project in Michigan was started after a woman dies in just such a situation.

Telephone reassurance provides a daily telephone contact for an older person who might otherwise have no outside contact for long periods of time.

Persons receiving telephone reassurance are called at a predetermined time each day. If the person does not answer, help is immediately sent to this home. Usually in the event of no answer, a neighbor, relative or nearby police or fire station is asked to make a personal check. Such details are worked out when a person begins receiving this service.

Telephone services have been credited with saving many lives by dispatching medical help in time. An alert caller, in one case, noticed a slight slurring of speech in a client she talked with regularly. Although the client reported no difficulties, the caller reported the slurred speech to her supervisor who sent someone to check the situation personally. The client had suffered a heart spasm and was rushed to the hospital — in time!

Telephone reassurance generally costs little in money and can be provided by callers of any age from teenagers to older people themselves. They are sponsored by a variety of organizations and agencies ranging from women's clubs to police departments.

Examples

In Nassau County, N.Y., residents of a home for the aged make calls to older people who live alone.

In Florida, 102 older persons who cannot leave their homes are called daily by 42 senior center members.

In Alburquerque, N.M., a hospital auxillary and the Business and Professional Women's Club make daily calls.

In Nebraska, the State Federation of Women's Clubs sponsors telephone reassurance.

In Ohio, six different churches cooperate in sponsoring a

telephone program.

Another type of telephone service is provided in Davenport, Iowa. Called "Dial-a-Listener", it provides a telephone number for an older person to call if he just wants to talk. Ten elderly professional people are the listeners. It has been outstandingly popular.

FRIENDLY VISITING

Friendly visiting has been called organized neighborliness because, in this kind of program, volunteers visit isolated home-bound older persons on a regular schedule once, or more often, a week. They do such things as play chess and cards, write letters, provide an arm to lean on during a shopping trip, and just sit and chat. The essential element is to provide continuing companionship for an elderly person who has no relative or friend able to do it.

This kind of visiting relieves loneliness of older people in a very real way. Older people themselves say such things as, "She has made my life over" ... "It makes me feel like I am still somebody worth talking to" ... "It gives me a chance to speak of things which are in my heart" ... "Her visit is something to look forward to."

Professional staff workers have observed that clients look better and take more interest in things outside themselves after receiving friendly visiting. Frequently there is improvement in actual physical condition or, at least, less absorption in illness.

Although the Visitor need not be a social worker or other professionally trained person he should receive some orientation from the sponsoring agency and some continuing supervision or consultation. Visitors come from a variety of backgrounds. Qualities that seem to mark all good friendly visitors are the ability to accept people as they are and a genuine friendliness plus commitment and reliability in visiting on a regular schedule. Older people themselves often prove most effective visitors. The ideal friendly visitor is born, not made.

Pioneer Services

Friendly visiting as an organized service began in Chicago in 1946. Social workers observed how extremely lonely many older clients were. Already swamped by caseloads, they wished for time to stay and chat with clients after their regular business was completed. The idea of asking volunteers to visit these isolated people grew out of this need.

The Volunteer Bureau of the Welfare Council of Metropolitan Chicago coordinates the program of recruitment, training, and referral of visitors. Public and private agencies requesting friendly visitors draw up job descriptions, acquaint visitors with agency purposes and programs, and establish time and place for consultation of volunteers with a professional member of the staff.

Greatly Needed

Friendly visiting is a service desired by many people in both rural and urban areas. It helps them to remain in their own homes, a goal shared by the great majority of older persons. When a survey was recently taken of older people in the Portland, Oregon, Model Cities Area, home visits to shut-ins and persons living alone topped the list of needs. It was even placed ahead of need for higher income and low cost transportation. ("Home visits" by Portland's definition included performance of some home chore and handyman type services as well as Friendly Visiting.)

Although many Friendly Visiting programs assign one volunteer to only one, or sometimes two clients, a school bus driver in Yampa Valley, Colorado, visits several older people every day. After delivering the children to school, he parks his bus and makes "rounds" dropping in to say hello to people until time to start the bus for the children's return trip.

In the YES (Youth Elderly Service) program of Fall River, Mass., one hundred volunteer high school girls and boys visit elderly residents in nine nursing homes.

In West Hartford, Conn., and San Francisco, Calif., high

school students take part in "Adopt-a-Grandparent" programs. They write letters, do errands, play cards and mostly talk with their "grandparents."

Texas "Roadrunner" Volunteers, Inc. of Austin visits residents of 43 nursing homes, provides transportation to the nursing homes for visitors who cannot provide their own, and takes groups of patients and visitors on outings.

IN-HOME SERVICES FOR OLDER PEOPLE

Living in their own homes is a great desire of many older people. Home services can help make this possible. Some older persons with chronic conditions need regular, continuing help with preparing meals, keeping the house tidy, and personal grooming. For others, help is needed only temporarily while they recover from an illness, or while the person who usually gives care is unable to do so.

Many older people may be quite able to handle normal household tasks, but need help with heavier chores such as washing walls, moving furniture, cleaning gutters and taking down storm windows. Accidents which permanently disable people often occur because homes lack minor necessary repairs.

Homemakers

Homemaker Service in many communities provides an alternative to institutionalization for individuals in need of some personal assistance. Usually sponsored or coordinated by a Visiting Nursing Association, welfare department, or other social agency, Homemaker Service can be useful to all persons without regard to income, social status, or other arbitrary limitation.

A homemaker is usually a mature woman with skills in home management and an instinctive understanding of human behavior. She usually has some basic training in simple home care of the sick but she is not a substitute for professional personnel such as a nurse or social worker. Neither is she a maid.

With professional supervision by nurses or social workers, Homemakers have helped many individuals to remain in familiar home surroundings. Even where older persons do not live alone, a Homemaker's services can lessen the stress on the person's usual caretaker, thereby avoiding unnecessary institutionalization and making life happier for the whole family.

Home Health Aides

Home Health Aides are paraprofessionals who meet a variety of out-of-hospital health needs. They are sometimes part of homemaker services personnel, or part of health service teams. Before Medicare was passed very few health insurance programs provided coverage for Home Health Services and there were relatively few Homemaker-Home Health Aide agencies. By 1970, however, 2300 Home Health agencies had qualified to participate in the medicare program. Studies indicate that physicians and patients who use Homemaker-Home Health services like them. Most professionals agree that there should be more such agencies offering a greater variety of in-home services.

Because a Homemaker-Home Health Aide is likely to be called into a home in time of crisis, and frequently will be substituting her judgment for that of the older person in her care, the training, reliability, and basic common sense of the worker must be assured by the sponsor of the service.

Many agencies and independent groups provide Homemaker-Home Health Aide service. Locally any such service should be officially recognized by local health and welfare councils, Visiting Nurse Associations, State welfare or social service departments, and State and local health departments.

The National Council of Homemaker-Home Health Aide Services, Inc., is presently developing accreditation standards for Homemaker-Home Health Aide agencies.

Other Home Services

Many communities have devised other organized ways to help older people to care for themselves and their households.

Earlham, Iowa, has shown that a small rural town can successfully provide home services economically to its senior citizens. The Earlham Care Program, since 1963, has provided homemakers to help with cleaning and cooking, and handymen to replace light bulbs, mow lawns, make small repairs, and put up storm windows for winter.

STEP (Service to Elderly Persons) in the State of Washington coordinates a program in which teenagers perform heavy household and gardening tasks. They move furniture, wash walls, mow lawns, spade gardens and help with other lifting chores.

Elder-Care, one of the SOS programs (Senior Opportunities and Services) funded by the Office of Economic Opportunity, includes housecleaning, marketing, meal preparation, and home repairs in its neighborhood service system for senior citizens, in Jasper, Alabama. Older persons employed by the Community Action Agency in Jasper provide these services.

Commmunity Activities for Senior Arkansans, CASA, sponsored by the Farmer's Union and funded by AoA and the U. S. Department of Labor used local senior citizens to provide in-home services. They repaired screens, steps and porches, brought in wood for a blind man, and cooked for the sick. Aides said they gained as much from this project as the people they helped.

Repairs-on-Wheels is a new volunteer service in Westmoreland County, Pennsylvania. Minor repairs are made to the homes of senior citizens who are not physically able to do it themselves. No federal or state funds are used.

The social benefits to both the individual and the community when institutionalization can be avoided are enormous. While precise figures on alternative costs are not available from most programs, the State of Nevada, which analyzed its costs after 2 years of Homemaker service, states that its Department of Welfare saved over $43,000 the first year of operation, and $65,000 the second year. It realized significant savings even for clients who received extremely high amounts of service. For instance, one woman was maintained in her own home at a total cost of $5,314.48. The alternative — nursing home care — would have cost $8,400.

New Jersey and Wisconsin have also anaslyzed the cost of homemaker services and found substantial savings over alternative care costs.

OPPORTUNITIES TO SERVE

Skills and experience, valuable to a community, are often ignored because of myths about aging. Although many older people need to be provided with services, hundreds of thousands of others need an opportunity to give service. In job after job across the country, wherever they have been hired or accepted as volunteers, older people have shown themselves dependable, capable, and willing workers. Yet, discrimination because of calendar age, bars many in both volunteer and employment programs.

Public Service

Many agencies of government, Federal, state, and local, sponsor or assist in funding programs using the services of older people as volunteers and paid workers. Many of these programs are "demonstrations" federally funded for a limited time, with the intention that programs which prove of value will be continued on a more permanent basis with local funding.

In the landmark Foster Grandparent Program initiated by AoA, older people with low incomes work with children in institutions such as schools for retarded or disturbed children, infant homes, temporary care centers, and convalescent hospitals. "Grandparents" do not replace regular staff, but establish a person-to-person relationship with a child, giving it the kind of love often missed in group-care settings. In return, "grandparents" receive an hourly stipend plus the affection and trust of the child.

Green Thumb and Green Light programs employ low-income men and women in rural sections to beautify public areas such as parks and roadsides, and to help local government and community services as aides in schools and libraries. Some provide outreach and Homemaker Service, make friendly visits and provide transportation. These projects are sponsored by the Farmers Union under a grant from the U. S. Department of

Labor.

Under another U. S. Department of Labor contract the American Association of Retired Persons and the National Retired Teachers Association have trained many older people in new skills and helped others brush up unused skills. In most cases, training was given by community service agencies such as the Red Cross or United Fund, with real work constitutiong the training mechanism. Trainees serve others while they learn.

Some Model Cities Areas have effectively employed older residents in day care centers thus allowing small children's parents to take jobs secure in the knowledge that their children are well cared for during the parents' absence. The children, the parents, and the older residents all benefit.

In the Seattle Model Cities Neighborhood, older men and women are employed to give direct service as Homemakers and handymen to other Model Neighborhood residents — serving both older persons and children. In Seattle, as in all Model Cities, older residents comprise a high proportion of the population.

The National Council of Senior Citizens employs older men and women as senior AIDES (Alert, Industrious, Dedicated, Energetic Service) in 21 projects from coast to coast under a Department of Labor contract. These senior citizens, who work 20 hours a week, perform a wide variety of community services, including low-cost meal preparation and outreach activizies. Many have found full-time jobs as a direct result of this project. The National Council on the Aging, Inc., operates a similar program with U. S. Department of Labor funding.

Help in Schools

Schools in many parts of the country are using older volunteers as a major community resource to provide children with educational enrichment.

In Winnetka, Illinois, older members of PAM (Project for Academic Motivation) meet children in a one-to-one relationship to discuss and experiment, work with small groups, or lecture before whole classes. They work with all school ages from elementary to senior grades and with children from a wide range of income and social backgrounds. A major contribution is the "revelation" to many children of the link between classroom work and its future use in "the real world" outside. With AoA demonstration fund help the program has spread throughout the State of Illinois and beyond through consultative help from PAM volunteers.

In Dade County (Florida) public schools, teacher aides are paid to perform a wide variety of non-instructional tasks which support the teacher, the pupil, and the schools in improving educational programs. Originally an AoA federally-funded research and demonstration project, these teacher aides have proven so valuable that Dade County has continued to hire them as regular employees after federal funding was discontinued.

Fill Community Needs

In Vermont, senior library aides, earning $1.60 an hour, make it possible for public libraries, particularly in the rural areas, to remain open longer, on more days. Book circulation has zoomed upward and students among others, are making increased use of library facilities. Interestingly, there is no absenteeism problem, even during the severest Vermont winters.

SERVE (Serve and Enrich Retirement by Volunteer Experience) of New York uses groups of older volunteers in state hospitals and schools for the mentally retarded. Some work with patients, some in the office, some help with other hospital duties. The group idea, both in recruitment and actual service is a major factor in the success of SERVE because the group experience itself brings benefits to older people. They make new friendships while riding together on the bus provided for them and gain a sense of belonging and *esprit de corps* sharing their experiences in group discussions.

SERVE began on Staten Island, N.Y., as an AoA demonstration project. It has proven so successful that the State of New York has continued to fund the project and has expanded it to include other locations through the State.

Senior citizens in two Michigan counties worked as tourist guides during the summer of 1970, showing 30,000 visitors the counties' scenic views and their good fishing and camping sites off the main roads. Many visitors stayed on an extra day or two and promised to vacation on the Michigan peninsula again because the guides made their vacations so pleasant.

Private Industry

John Deere Tractor Company hired 50 of its former employees also as tour guides in its Waterloo, Iowa plant. These retirees escort 14,000 tourists a year through the plant. And when John Deere Co. holds a meeting in Waterloo for its international sales representatives, the guides help give the salesmen their orientation. They are naturals as guides because they not only know about the plant and tractor building processes, but they also care deeply about the company's "image."

Some companies, however, fear that hiring older workers will create problems with established retirement plans or health insurance. Since many older people prefer to work only part-time, ways to meet these situations have been devised by special employment and referral services especially for older people. Some are private profit making firms, others are volunteer and community agencies.

Obstacles Overcome

The hiring, payroll and paperwork for the John Deere guides, for example, are handled by Manpower, Inc., the national "temporaries' agency." Because the guides are actually employed by Manpower which contracts their services to John Deere no retirement benefits are affected.

One of the private firms specializing in older employees is Mature Temps, Inc. with offices in at least 13 major cities, it places older people in temporary jobs on a contract basis. Mature Temps, Inc., pays their salary, social security, and insurance. These programs have been so successful that some Temps offices have been having difficulty in hiring enough people to fill all their potential contracts. Mature Temps reports that many companies are so pleased with their employees that they are

asking to hire them permanently. One new York firm employs 50
Mature Temps every month.

Retirement Jobs, Inc., of San Jose, California, has placed over
5,000 older men and women in jobs since its beginning in 1963.
"RJ" now has five offices serving Santa Clara, San Mateo and San
Francisco counties. It estimates its members earn between
$150,000 and $200,000 in one year putting several times that
amount in purchasing power back into the community. No fees
are charged.

A group of retirees in Norwalk, Connecticut, with AoA help,
organized the Senior Personnel Placement Bureau in 1966. They
have placed persons in jobs paying from $1.75 per hour to $10,000
a year. Like other senior employment agencies the Bureau will
pay a worker directly under a contract arrangement.

In 8 years experience in finding jobs for older people, the Over-
60 Employment Counseling Service of Maryland, Inc., has placed
3042 seniors in 4082 separate jobs. With a small executive staff and
the help of many volunteers, it charges no fee to either job-seeker
or employer. Expenses of the agency are met through voluntary
contributions from corporations, industrial and commercial
concerns, foundations and individuals. Over-60 figures show it
costs $22.20 and an average of 15 hours work per placement.

Baltimore seniors have been placed in such jobs as director of
promotion and fund raising for a hospital, business manager for a
private school, live-in companion, and clerical positions. The
agency has difficulty finding enough bookkeepers to fill requests.

A Comprehensive County-Wide Program

Under the sponsorship of the Montgomery County Federation
of Women's Clubs, Senior Home Craftsmen and Good Neighbor
Family Aides in Montromery County, Maryland, work in their
own neighborhoods. In a sprawling suburban area such as this
county, where extensive travel time could make part-time work
prohibitive, this is important.

Senior Home Craftsmen are men who do minor home repairs
such as replacing faucet washers, fixing locks, painting,
wallpaper hanging, and other handyman jobs which are too

small for commercial firms. Potential conflict with commercial businesses has been resolved by the Over-60 Counseling and Employment Service, the Washington Building Trades Council representing union members, and the Suburban Maryland Home builders Association representing commercial contractors.

All agree that the senior craftsmen could reasonably charge about half the going hourly rate because they would not necessarily work as fast as union members, and because they might be unwilling to do everything that is required of a union workman such as heavy lifting or working high above the ground. It was also agreed that the senior craftsmen would limit themselves to small home repair jobs which would not be profitable to commercial contractors.

There is no absolute time or dollar maximum on jobs because one homeowner might want several small jobs such as repairing screens, painting one room, or replacing stairs which would amount to considerable time and money but would still be unprofitable to a contractor. The rule of reasonableness and a common understanding of the position of both the senior craftsmen and commercial contractors and unions govern. There have been no difficulties with this gentleman's agreement.

Most of the men can do these jobs because they have had a lifetime of keeping their own homes in good repair. A few have had careers as professional carpenters or bricklayers but no longer can or want to work full time at such strenuous jobs. One handyman teaches a home repair course at the local YWCA to county residents who want to learn to do minor repair themselves. The Adult Education Department of the public schools has also set up a class for men who want to be senior craftsmen but feel that they need some instruction.

The Good Neighbor Family Aides are women who have been homemakers most of their lives and who can offer aid to other older persons or families who need help in caring for a home. The women receive training at no cost to them in the local Red Cross chapter house. A Red Cross nurse teaches home nursing skills, the State university extension agent teaches home economics, and a local psychiatrist who specializes in geriatrics, volunteers his time to give insight on care of elderly persons.

Members of the Federation provide transportation within the county to the Red Cross chapter house for the training. People from adjoining Maryland counties and the adjoining State of Virginia and the District of Columbia have also taken this training and are now working in their own communities.

The Aides have had enthusiastic acceptance by the community with the Over-60 Counseling Service receiving about 12 requests for ever one it is able to fill. The Service frequently receives letters of gratitude from families who have benefited. Mothers of small children or adults who care for an elderly person in their homes are able to take short vacations knowing that their family responsibilities are in capable hands.

Although income, educational level and social position of the Aides vary widely, a study of the Aides done by a graduate student shows need for additional income as most of the Aides' primary reason for working. A high percentage, however, also indicated the desire to be involved in the community, to fill a real need, and to have freedom to schedule working hours as they wish as reasons for being Aides.

OUTREACH SERVICES

Remaining hidden from the social life and knowledge of their community, many older people do not know of the opportunities available to them. Their community does not realize their need, and indeed, sometimes it doesn't know they exist.

For these reasons it is often desirable and necessary to seek out older people to make sure they know what services are available and where they can call for help. This kind of program, often called "Outreach," can be organized by almost any group or agency with volunteers who have some special training, in much the same way that Medicare Alert sought out older people to tell them about Medicare when that program began.

Outreach volunteers can be older people themselves. Often they are the most effective. Some communities pay outreach workers for time and services; all should pay their transportation and other expenses.

Sometimes outreach can be provided by active senior centers

through the establishment of satellite neighborhood centers. These neighborhood offshoots can draw previously isolated older people into neighborhood activity.

Project FIND (Friendless, Isolated, Needy, or Disabled) conducted from August 1967 through November 1968 by the National Council on Aging and the Office of Economic Opportunity, made surveys of 12 communities using aides, ranging in age from 50 to 85. The aides found isolated persons and referred those who needed help to services available in the community. If needed services were not available, the aides tried to secure volunteer help, especially when the need was severe. On of the significant discoveries of FIND was that many persons eligible for Social Security were not receiving it. The fact, that 28,079 referrals were made to existing services and 24,124 unavailable services were needed, clearly establishes a reason for outreach.

In some places television and radio programs for, about, and by older people, have provided a special kind of outreach. Some of these maintain a telephone answering service or include in their programming persons who will answer questions on the air. Because the older viewers have confidence in the programs, even extremely isolated individuals do seek and accept information which they would resist or not seek from a social agency which was strange to them. An aggressive campaign to make people aware of the program's existence is essential to the success of this type of program.

Outreach should be considered as part of every program established for older persons. Often those who need service most are least likely to be aware of potential assistance. These people are not usually reached by standard mass media communication channels. Cut off from their communities by high costs and almost complete lack of transportation, they must be actively sought out and personally invited to participate in programs.

INFORMATION AND REFERRAL SERVICES

Many communities need information and referral centers to link older persons in need of services with the services already available in their communities. There are, today, a distressingly large number of elderly Americans for whom adequate services exist at the community level who have failed to connect with the service system.

Almost daily, people are found in financial crises who don't know they are eligible for Social Security, or how to apply for it! Sometimes people do try to find assistance. But after being referred from one agency to another, they despair of finding the right one and give up.

For these reasons, follow-up to see that clients are properly referred and receive needed services should be an integral part of any information and referral service.

In addition to linking persons in need with available service, information and referral programs can identify unmet needs and gaps in community services.

Central information and referral service can be offered as a component of health or welfare programs by a variety of public or private organizations. Or it can be an independent service cooperating with all established services and agencies.

The State of Maryland, for instance, has established on toll-free phone number for the entire State from which seniors can get information. A specialist is on duty from 9 to 5, Mondays through Fridays. Calls during other hours are recorded and returned the next working day.

Westchester County, N. Y., gives information and referral from a toll-free number which serves its entire area.

A 6-county area in Kansas and Missouri began an information and referral service as an alternative to a survey to find what services were wanted and needed. In addition to giving the desired information on referral, the staff kept records on callers so that data such as sex, age, occupation, geographic location, and service requested could be quickly ascertained.

In spite of the fact that there were at least 450 agencies in the area meeting health and welfare needs, the information and referral service identified many gaps in service.

New Resources

A valuable resource for many agencies is a new book developed under the auspices of the Legislative Research Center of the University of Michigan Law School and the National Council of Senior Citizens under a grant from the Office of Economic Opportunity. Called a "Handbook of Model State Statutes," it deals with the areas of living accommodations, consumer aid and protection, age discrimination, protective and supportive services, rate and fee reductions, and tax relief.

The book has received wide circulation to OEO legal service programs, State legislators, senior citizen organizations, OEO community action agencies, State commissions on aging, and law school libraries. It may be available for study locally from one of these groups.

The Administration on Aging is at present developing a nationwide network of information and referral programs as one of its major research and demonstration projects under Title IV of the Older Americans Act.

An exceptional film on information and referral values and the success of a good program for people of all ages is *Tell Me Where To Turn*. It was produced by the Public Affairs Committee with grant support from the U. S. Public Health Service.

REFERENCES

Transportation

Publications

AoA Administrative Paper No. 20: *Increasing Mobility Among Isolated Older People*. (YMCA of Metropolitan Chicago)

AoA Administrative Paper No. 23: *Elderly Ridership and Reduced Transit Fares: The New York Experience*.

AoA Administrative Paper No. 30: *Elderly Ridership and Reduced Transit Fares:* The Chicago Experience.

AoA Position Paper: Mobility, Transportation and Aging.

Older Americans and Transportation: A Crisis in Mobility. A report by the U.S. Senate Special Committee on Aging, Superintendent of Documents, U. S. Government Printing Office, Washington, D. C. 204202. Price 50 cents.

The Minibus Brings Sparkle to Little House. Stanford Research Institute, Menlo Park, California 94025.

Developing Transportation Services for Older People. Senior Opportunities and Services, Technical Assistance Monograph No. 4 (Includes STRIDE and CAA project in Missouri.) Office of Older Persons Programs, Office of Economic Opportunity, 1200 19th Street, N.W., Washington, D. C. 20506.

Senior Citizen Bus Transportation Project in Prince George's County, Maryland. Division of Services and Programs for the Aging, 9171 Central Avenue, Hampton Hall, Capitol Heights, Maryland 20027.

People and Organizations

Providence, Rhode Island, Leonard E. Walker, Project Director, Urban League, 131 Washington St., Providence, R. I. 02903.

Waynesboro, Virginia, Doris Anne Miller, Director, Central Shenandoah Aging Program. 301 Walnut, Waynesboro, Virginia.

South Routt County, Colorado, W. N. Leuthauser, Division of Services for the Aging, State Department of Social Services, 1575 Sherman Street, Denver, Colorado 80203.

STRIDE and CAA Project in Missouri and any other transportation project funded by OEO Irven Eitreim, Office of Older Persons/Operations, Office of Economic Opportunity, 1200 19th St., N.W. Washington, D.C. 20506.

Texas "Roadrunner" Volunteers, Inc., Esther Trekell, CVC, 4501 Manchaca Road, Austin, Texas 78745.

YMCA Senior Citizens Mobile Service, John H. Bell, Project Director, 3763 South Wabash Avenue, Chicago, Illinois 60653.

Senior Center

Publications

AoA No. 906: *A Project Report on a Centralized Comprehensive Program.* (Nashville, Tennessee, Senior Citizens, Inc.)

AoA No. 908: *A Project Report on Statewide Community Organization.* (North Dakota Lutheran Welfare Society).

AoA Patterns for Progress No. 17: *A Rural County Cares For Its Aging.* (Aiken County, Minnesota, Report).

AoA Patterns for Progress No. 18: *Brighter Vistas: Church Programs for Older Adults.* (St. Luke's Methodist Church, Oklahoma City, Oklahoma).

Directory of Senior Citizens Centers. Lists 1200 centers throughout the country which are open three or more days a week. Superintendent of Documents, U. S. Government Printing Office, Washington, D. C. 20402 ($2 per copy).

People and Organizations

Hodson Senior Center, Abbe Hacker, Director, Division of Senior Centers, 109 E.

16th St., New York, N.Y. 10003.

Knowles Senior Citizens Center, Sebastian Tine, Senior Citizens, Inc., 1801 Broadway, Nashville, Tennessee 37203.

Little House Senior Center, Jean Von Ezdorf, Executive Director, 800 Middle Avenue, Menlo Park, California 94025.

National Institute of Senior Centers, NCOA, 1828 L. Street, N.W., Washington, D.C. 20036.

Plymouth Senior Citizens Center, Mildred M. Krez, Director, 128 E. Mill Street, Plymouth, Wisconsin 53073.

Nutrition

Publications

AoA Position Paper: Nutrition for Older Americans: *Demonstration Program Experience,* 1970.

AoA Administrative Paper No. 14, *Older People's Response to a Nutrition Program.* Henry Street Settlement House, New York, New York.

AoA Administrative Paper No. 14-A, *Nutrition for Inner-City Aged.* Urban League, Washington, D. C.

AoA Administrative Paper 14-B, *A Survey of Elderly Volunteers in a Nutrition Program.* Community Action Program, Western, Idaho.

AoA Administrative Paper 14-C: *Neighborhood-Kitchen Meal for the Aging Poor.* Murphy-Blair area, St. Louis, Missouri.

AoA Administrative Paper No. 14-D: *Nutrition and Health-Screening Services to the Aging.* YM-YWCAs of Greater New York City.

AoA Administrative Paper No. 14-E: *Columbia Club — A Nutrition Demonstration Project for Low Income Elderly.*

Baltimore Meals-on Wheels Manual. Baltimore Meals-on-Wheels, Inc., 1509 Park Avenue, Baltimore, Maryland 21201. For sale at $4 per copy.

Mealtime Manual for the Aged and Handicapped. Essandess Special Editions, Simon & Shuster, Inc., 630 Fifth Avenue, New York, New York 10020. For sale at $2 per copy. May also be available at local bookstore or library.

People and Organizations

Baltimore Meals-on-Wheels, Inc., Peggy Sheeler, Executive Director, 1509 Park Avenue, Baltimore, Maryland 21201.

Center for Community Research, Douglas Holmes, Ph.D., Director, 33 West 60th Street, New York, New York 10023 (National Survey of Home Delivered Meals).

SAMS (and any other nutrition program funded by AoA,) Jeanette Pelcovits, Nutrition Specialist on Aging, Administration on Aging, 330 C Street S.W., Washington, D. C. 20201.

State of Massachusetts, John H. Crain, Jr., Director, Office of Services to Older Americans, 141 Milk Street, Boston, Massachusetts 02109.

Dr. Dorothy Rowe, Department of Home Economics, Madison College, Harrisonburg, Va.

Telephone Reassurance

Publications

Guidelines for a Telephone Reassurance Program, Report of the Michigan Program, available from AoA.

Suggestions for Operating a Ring-a-Day Telephone Reassurance Program. Eda R. Kaye, Director, Nassau County Office for the Aging, 33 Willis Avenue, Mineola, New York 11501.

Teleclub of Bay Village: An Organization Guide, 31410 Carlton Drive, Bay Village, Ohio 44140.

Telephone Reassurance, a People to People Program, Public Information Office, State of Nebraska Advisory Committee on Aging, State House Station 94784, Lincoln, Nebraska 68509.

People and Organizations

Dial-a-Listener, Lois Haecker, Lend-a-Hand Building, 105 South Main Street, Davenport, Iowa, 52801.

Florida Senior Center, Paul B. Richardson, Executive Director, Volusia County Citizens Advisory Council on Aging, Inc., 524 South Beach Street, Daytona, Florida 32014.

Friendly Visiting

Publications

Why Friendly Visiting? International Ladies Garment Workers' Union, Retiree Service Department, 301 West 52nd Street, New York, New York 10019.

People and Organizations

Texas "Roadrunner" Volunteers, Inc., Esther Trekell, CVC, 4501 Manchaca Road, Austin, Texas 78745.

Welfare Council of Metropolitan Chicago, Maxine E. Miller, Executive Director, 123 W. Madison Street, Chicago, Illinois 60602.

Yampa Valley, W. N. Leuthauser, Division of Services for the Aging, State Department of Social Services, 1575 Sherman Street, Denver, Colorado 80203.

YES Program, Dorothy Wahl, RATE, Family Service Association, 101 Rock Street, Fall River, Massachusetts 02720.

In-Home Services

Publications

AoA Fact Sheet on Homemaker Services for Older People. Brief history of homemaker services, definition, present problems and issues.

Directory of Homemaker-Home Health Aide Services, National Council for Homemaker Services, Inc. (Lists all agencies which provide homemaker-home health aide services. Includes age groups served.) (Available from AoA).

National Capital Area Homemaker Service Training Manual, Homemaker Service of the National Capital Area, Inc., Washington, D. C. (Available from AoA).

Public Health Reports: Sept. 1970, Vol. 85, No. 9. Contains special section on health aides. HSMA, Room 4B-44, Parklawn Bldg, 5600 Fishers Lane, Rockville, Maryland 30852.

Standards for Homemaker — Home Health Aide Services. Available from the National Council for Homemaker Services, Inc., 1790 Broadway, N.Y., N.Y. 10019. For sale at $1 per copy.

People and Organizations

Elder-Care (and all other In Home Services funded by OEO.) Irven Eitreim, Office of Older Persons/Operations, Office of Economic Opportunity, 1200 19th St., N.W., Washington, D. C. 20506.

National Council of Homemaker-Home Health Aide Services, Inc., Florence Moore, Executive Director, 1740 Broadway, New York, New York 10019.

Nevada State Welfare Department, Maxine Beck, Coordinator, Homemaker Services, Carson City, Nevada, 89701. (For specific questions on data and/or methods used in this cost analysis study.)

Repairs-on-Wheels, William T. Zalot, 116 W. Otterman St., Greensburg, Pennsylvania 15601.

STEP, Sally Wren, Director, South Snohomish County Senior Center, 220 Railroad Ave., Edmonds, Washington 98020.

Opportunities to Serve

Publications

AoA Fact Sheet: Employment and Volunteer Opportunities for Older Americans: Programs of the Federal Government.

AoA No. 145: *Aging Magazine* reprint, "Older People as a Resource." Reports on variety of work, employment and volunteer projects including PAM, SERVE, and Vermont Library Aides.

AoA No. 904: *A Project Report on Employment Referral* (Norwalk, Connecticut report).

AoA No. 905: *A Project Report on Group Volunteer Service* (Report on SERVE).

SRS-AOA No. 155-70: *Foster Grandparent Program.*

An Overview of the NRTA-AARP Senior Community Service Aides Project. Available from NRTA-AARP, 1225 Connecticut Avenue, N.W., Washington, D. C. 20036.

Improving With Age. Reprint from Wall Street Journal, Nov. 2, 1970. Available from AoA.

Jobs for the Retired. Available from Retirement Jobs, Inc., 161 N. First St., San Jose, California 95113.

The Older Worker as a Volunteer. Report to the Governor on the Older Worker Program... 1968, State of California. Available from Dept. of Human Resources, 800 Capitol Mall, Sacramento, California 95814.

People and Organizations

Action (The new Federal Volunteer agency administering Peace Corps, Vista, Score, Foster Grandparent Program, RSVP, etc. after July 1, 1971), 806 Connecticut Avenue, Washington, D. C. 20525.

Baltimore Over-60 Employment Counseling Service, Arthur Wyatt, Executive Director, 309 N Charles St., Baltimore, Maryland 21201.

John Deere Tour Guides, Marilyn Kleist, Manager, Manpower, Inc. 313 W. 4th Street, Waterloo, Iowa, 50701.

Mature Temps, Inc., Barry K. Zern, President, 521 Fifth Avenue, N.Y., N.Y. 10017.

Michigan Summer Tour Guides, Thomas Vizanko, Director, Community Action Agency, P.O. Box 188, Ironwood, Michigan 49338.

Montgomery County Over-60 Counseling and Employment Service of the Montgomery County Federation of Women's Clubs, Gladys Sprinkle, Director, 4707 Norwood Drive, Chevy Chase, Maryland 20015.

PAM, Howard Bede, Winnetka Public Schools, 1155 Oak Street, Winnetka, Ill., 60096.

Senior AIDES, William R. Hutton, Executive Director, National Council of Senior Citizens, 1627 K Street, N.W., Washington, D. C. 20006.

Senior Community Service Project, National Council on the Aging, Inc., 1828 L St., N.W., Suite 808, Washington, D. C. 20036.

SERVE, Janet Sainer, Community Service Society, 105 East 22nd St., N.Y., N.Y. 10010.

Teacher Aides, Lillian Battle, Department of Staff Development, Dade County Schools, Northeast 19th St., Miami, Florida 33132.

Green Thumb — Green Light, Blue Carstenson, National Director Farmers

Union, 1012 14th Street, N.W. Suite 1200, Washington, D. C. 20005.

Outreach

Publications

AoA Administrative Paper No. 16: *Passing Time: Older People in Public Places.*
AoA Administrative Paper No. 22: *Downward Mobility in Old Age.*
AoA Administrative Paper No. 24: *Social Isolation and Widows of Blue Collar Workers.*
AoA Administrative Paper No. 28: *Geriatric Psychiatry: Out-patients and the Community.*
AoA Position Paper: *Protective Services.*
The Golden Years...A Tarnished Myth, Available from National Council on the Aging, 1828 L St. N.W., Washington, D. C. 20036.

People and Organizations

Dr. John C. Schwarzwalder, General Manager, 1640 TCA-ETV-TV, Como Avenue, St. Paul, Minnesota 55108 (Seminar for Seniors).
The Time of Our Lives, a regional television program for older people, Michael Ziegler, Assistant Manager for Programming, WITF-TV, South Central Broadcasting Council, Community Center Building, P. O. Box 2, Hershey, Pennsylvania 17033.

Information and Referral

Publications

AoA No. 903: What Churches Can Do — Inter-Faith Opportunity Center (Hartford, Conn.).
AoA No. 907: *A Project Report on Countywide Information and Referral* (Westchester County, N.Y.).
Information and Referral Centers: A Functional Analysis, Institute for Interdisciplinary Studies of the American Rehabilitation Foundation, Minneapolis, Minnesota. (Available from AoA).
Information and Referral Manuals: A series of "how to's" on various facets of the service, Institute for Interdisciplinary Studies of the American Rehabilitation Foundation, Minneapolis, Minnesota. (Available from AoA).
Legislative Approaches to the Problems of the Elderly: A Handibook of Model State Statues. Available from Legal Research and Services for the Elderly, National Council of Senior Citizens, 1627 K Street, N.W., Washington, D.C. 20006. No charge to those working with elderly poor.

Film

Tell Me Where To Turn — A 26 1/2-minute 16mm color and sound film on setting up information and referral services in a community. For rental $10. For purchase $150. Public Affairs Committee, Inc., 381 Park Avenue, South, New York, New York 10016.

CHAPTER 2

COUNSELING WITH
THE OLDER AMERICAN

JOHN G. CULL and RICHARD E. HARDY

DEFINITION OF THE OLDER AMERICAN
EMOTIONAL ASPECTS OF AGING
PSYCHOLOGICAL ASPECTS OF AGING
EMPLOYMENT NEEDS OF THE AGING PERSON
SOCIAL NEEDS OF THE AGING PERSON

DEFINITION OF THE OLDER AMERICAN

THE purpose of this chapter is to outline some of the concerns to be considered in counseling with older Americans. It will cover some of the emotional, psychological, employment, and social needs of these individuals. Before looking at these specific areas, it would be appropriate to identify this segment of our population. In counseling and rehabilitation psychology, we tend to be quite exact in our functional descriptions or definitions of a disability group. For example, in mental illness there are numerous specific diagnostic categories which describe the psychological function of the individual; in cardiac involvement there is the functional heart classification; almost all state education and rehabilitation agencies use a rather specific range of IQ to define mental retardation, and IQ is a quantified approach to describing intellectual function; however, the term "older Americans" is filled with ambiguity. We use many other terms which are just as inadequate — the aged, the aging, senior citizens, geriatrics, golden-agers and many others. Not only are the names for this segment of our population indefinite and inadequate, the definitions are just as confusing. Almost all the definitions use age rather than function as the criterion. As many will recognize this is foreign to professionals involved in vocational rehabilitation since we pride ourselves on taking the humanistic or functional approach to individuals.

Most professional counselors in rehabilitation psychology prefer the term industrial gerontology or the industrial geriatric. According to Norman Sprague (1970), industrial gerontology is the study of the employment and retirement problems of middle-aged and older workers. It is the science of aging and work.

Industrial gerontology begins where age *per se* becomes a handicap to employment. Age discrimination in employment may start as early as thirty-five or forty in some industries and occupations, and it begins to take on major dimensions at age forty-five. Federal and state legislation impose age discrimination in employment policies generally around the ages of forty-to sixty-five. However, as in other disability areas of vocational rehabilitation, this condition (age) becomes a factor of concern only when it constitutes a handicap to employment.

Industrial gerontology is concerned with aptitude testing, job counseling, vocational training, and placement. It is concerned with job adjustment, job assignment and reassignment, retention on the job, redesign of the work requirements, vocational motivation, and mobility.

The similarity between the concerns of industrial gerontology and rehabilitation psychology and the degree of overlapping in these two areas are impressive. So programs in industrial gerontology are highly significant to the individuals charged with responsibilities for program planning and development in rehabilitation as well as the professional practitioner in the field.

Before discussing the specific needs of this segment of our population as outlined above, the authors would like to state a basic position which we feel most of us all accept but often forget. The similarities between any section of our population and the population as a whole are much greater than the dissimilarities. The industrial geriatric or "older American is more like than unlike the clients on our existing case loads. Programatic changes which are needed to adapt our services to this population will be minor and tend to be changes in emphasis rather than changes in direction.

EMOTIONAL ASPECTS OF AGING

A very interesting trend has occurred in our culture which has resulted in creating emotional needs for the "older American"; age is no longer related to conformity behavior (Cull, 1970). Traditionally we have revered our elders. In our culture we can see this reverence in the admonishments of the Old Testament. In the Indo Iranian and Hindu cultures we can turn to the *Rig Vedas*, *The Upanashads*, and the *Bhagavad-Gita* for the same admonishments. Since the beginning of time, cultures and societies have turned to their elders for judgments, decisions, values, and mores. The elders have determined the future of the tribe, culture, or society. This has been true universally until the past generation. The current generation of elders have been socially, economically, and vocationally emasculated. They have become a lost generation. They grew up expecting, and with every reason to expect, to mature into a role of influence in our culture. This is a very enviable role and one generally anticipated with a degree of eagerness. To become an elder had meaning, purpose, rewards, and status.

However, after the revolution in technology we now turn to younger, more aggressive, more highly trained individuals to make decisions. The demands for speed and innovation are two factors which have robbed older people of what they viewed as a birthright. Everything which smacks of seniority is under fire — even the committee hierarchy in Congress.

The result is this lost generation of elders have become confused, disoriented, relegated to an inferior role with a great amount of condescending expressions of concern. Rather than arriving at a state which would bring status and reverence and one filled with meaning and purpose, they have been pushed to early retirement, then isolated and forgotten. No wonder many are concerned, bitter, and resentful.

The most important need this group of individuals has is to feel useful. While much can be said for our new sophisticated decision-making theories, there is a great manpower pool of years of experience going to waste. This pool of manpower should be mobilized by our workshops for the benefit of both parties.

While production and income supplementation will solve some of the problems of the aging, the workshop can solve many others. In workshop operations, it has been found that if older workers are placed with younger retardates, the production of both groups increases and the discipline problems with the retarded youngsters are reduced. This arrangement also seems to be an effective motivating factor for the older worker. Life is becoming more meaningful for them — they are more useful.

PSYCHOLOGICAL ASPECTS OF AGING

When we think of the psychological aspects of aging, we almost automatically think of reduced intellectual ability. Almost all research studies between Galton's in 1883 up to Lorges in 1947 have indicated there is a decline in intelligence with age. The decline was supposed to be progressive beginning after a peak at age eighteen to twenty-five. However, more recent studies indicate this is not the case. It appears as if there is a plateau established at approximately age twenty-four to twenty-five. This plateau is stable until about age seventy. The objections to decline in intellectual abilities center around (a) the speeded nature of the tests and the decline of the individual's reaction time as opposed to intelligence, (b) the scores being dependent upon acquired and stored knowledge and older subjects being more remote from the time of schooling and having less schooling, and (c) the tests being constructed so they are more appropriate to younger subjects than older subjects. There is little if any reliable evidence that the older individual undergoes significant intellectual decline.

Testing deficits may be explained by lack of motivation, lowered reaction time, lack of familiarity with the testing orientation, as well as the considerations above.

A second factor to consider under psychological aspects of aging is the pathological mental conditions among the aged. This factor is probably the largest precluding factor in vocational rehabilitation's accepting and serving the aging population. There are statistics which support the position that age invariably brings on mental aberrations. During the last third of a century the admission rate of geriatrics in our state hospitals has zoomed.

There are many articles now appearing in the literature which indicate the state hospital geriatric wards are serving more as human warehouses and foster homes than bona fide treatment facilities. The high rate of admissions is partially explained by social and cultural factors rather than emotional factors. Due to the removal of much of the stigma attached to mental illness, many adults have older relatives committed on the slightest pretexts since this is a convenient solution to a social problem.

We are not trying to explain away the problems of the aging. Some are very serious and need the attention and concern of all of us; however, the problem is not of the magnitude we in vocational rehabilitation suppose. In the past we have felt the problems were insurmountable so we ignored them. The life expectancy for this attitude is indeed very short. It is incumbent on us as professionals to understand the problems of these people and mobilize our efforts to solve them.

In the psychological aspects of aging, one explanation of the increased incidence of a type of mental illness lies in the role they are required to accept. The current life style in our culture leads toward older citizens feeling much less secure, unhappy, nonproductive; they generally live in a home situation in which they have at best an ill-defined role; there is a feeling of dependence rather than independence which leads to self-respect. Their future is narrowing, constricting, and bleak with a diminishing health status (physical and emotional).

The last factor we will discuss in the psychological aspects of aging related to rehabilitation psychology is the psychological set of the older individual. All of us view ourselves as workers. If we become unemployed, we still tend to view ourselves as workers and as such are capable of work. The longer we are unemployed the more narrowed and rigid our view of our capabilities of working become. While employed, our psychological set relative to our capabilities for work is highly flexible. We feel we can do our job and many variations of our job in many different locations. The longer we are out of work the more rigid our psychological set of ourselves as workers becomes, until finally we become convinced we are no longer workers. This is very obvious among the coal miners of Appalachia. They can function only as coal miners in their local area. Since there are no jobs, they are unemployable. They no longer view themselves as workers.

This phenomenon is particularly appropriate with the aging. The longer they have been unemployed and the more they felt pushed out of their last job, the less they will characterize themselves as "a worker" or productive individual. Since the older individual has a rather strong need to be considered a useful person, but is unable to do so, his psychological adjustment to aging will be quite difficult.

EMPLOYMENT NEEDS OF THE AGING PERSON

Employment fulfills many functions and needs for all of us. As individuals we are what we do. In our culture we are identified by what we do for a living. Our economic status, self-concept, social status, friends, and community activities are to a great extent determined by our jobs. All of these factors which have direct bearing upon personality integration deteriorate in unemployment.

In the face of economic inflation, more and more concern is being expressed relative to retirement programs which provide fixed incomes. The inflationary spiral which we have had in this country for the last decade has seriously jeopardized or destroyed the stability of fixed-income retirement plans.

Therefore, the employment needs of the aging are two faceted — first, employment supplies many social and psychological needs which are essential to the individual and secondly, and more mundanely, employment needs of the aging include the provision for basic subsistence.

The productive older worker is interested, in many cases, in supplementing his fixed retirement income; therefore, his employment needs are uniquely adapted to part-time work or work involving a piece rate structure. His interests and vocational and production capabilities can be developed to the point of performing a diversity of subcontract work; and, if properly planned programs are instituted, a group of older Americans could attract national industrial contract work on a long term basis.

Work also can meet the social and psychological aspects of employment needs of older workers who have solved the problems of basic subsistence. For most bright, alert, aggressive retired persons, retirement, unless impeccably planned, soon begins to pall. The avocational pursuits which held so much attraction on the "pre" side of retirement soon become stultifying and deadly on the "past" side of retirement. Fishing, bridge, hiking and so forth soon fail to fill the void left by the demands and rewards of employment. Consequently, many retirees are looking for an opportunity to utilize the talents, abilities and proficiencies they have developed and perfected over many years of employment.

We are amazed that businesses have failed to adapt the SCORE concept (Service Corps of Retired Executives) on the local level. We feel these people represent a vast untapped reservoir of manpower in our communities. In some limited situations business have solicited volunteers composed of retired teachers to teach remedial subjects, but we have in our communities retired workers who were supervisors, foremen, managers, and executives concerned with purchasing, marketing, production, accounting, plant layout, and efficiency, and contract procurement — the same concerns we in workshop administration have. We believe a business administration can be highly self-serving and still meet some of the employment needs of retired workers by developing a program to utilize these people's talents in the operation, development, and administration of the industry.

They can be used on a continuing volunteer basis in areas such as staff development, production supervision, quality control, or on a consultative basis for marketing, contract procurement, et cetera. We feel this approach will gain the business not only improved efficiency in operations and administration but a wider base and greater degree of community support for its programs.

SOCIAL NEEDS OF THE AGING PERSON

It is difficult to separate the social needs of the aging from the other needs discussed above. Almost all of the needs outlined above have direct social implications.

The social needs of the aging, as well as other needs, are the same as for all populations. They need satisfying relationships with their peer groups, security in interpersonal relations (they need to know who they are and have a sense of identity), recognition for achievement and acceptance.

Generally, the aging process is also an isolating process. As people grow old and retire from work, their environment shrinks drastically until, in many instances, the individual withdraws into isolation. In this situation he becomes highly ego-oriented, selfish, and preoccupied with himself and his bodily functions to the point of becoming hypochondriacal. If the social needs of the individual continually fail to be fulfilled, this psychological and physiological deterioration will continue. Once established, this pattern of isolationism is extremely difficult to break since chronic behavior in the aged is relatively easy to establish and the drive for change and new experiences is subdued in them. Individuals in this social isolation system are so obvious or noticeable, regretfully they form the stereotype we have of the older persons. This is an unfair stereotype; but as all stereotypes, it is a highly persistent image highly impervious to change.

Most of the suggestions made above regarding meeting the various needs of the aging will also meet the social needs of the aging.

There are some specific programs of which the counselor should be aware in working with the older American. These programs are designed specifically to overcome the isolationism forces of aging. The tools we have to combat this dreadful isolation for older people exists at least in part in every community (DHEW, 1973). Some of these services specifically include transportation especially adapted to the physical needs of older people, adapted to their time tables, to the routes that will take them where they need and wish to go at a cost they can afford in spite of lowered incomes; senior centers which reach out with real services as well as recreation to bring people into the action center of the community's life; nutrition programs which provide meals for older people and social settings so they may gain friendship, social contacts, education and activity as well as improvement in health through proper nutrition; opportunities in paid employment and in volunteer activities to serve others thus in turn provides chances to be needed the most necessary of human requirements; and home services to make independent living more possible. Older people are not all isolated for the same reasons and they do not all need the same services. Often one service in itself is useless without a companion service. Many excellent health or recreation programs for example are not fully used by older persons because they lack transportation to reach them. Sometimes an older person not only needs transportation to a welfare department office or a health clinic but also needs someone to accompany him and stay with him to see that he gets the service he is entitled to, and to see that he understands what is being done. A counselor should realize that counseling services for this type of client in isolation from other services is wasted effort. Rarely can the service of counseling exclusively be used to solve the multiplicity of problems facing the older American.

Senior centers are places where older persons can come together for a variety of activities and programs. These range from just sitting and talking or playing cards to professionally directed hobby and group activities. Some centers provide counseling services to help individuals make better use of personal and community resources. Some assume responsibility for encouraging other community agencies to provide more help to senior citizens. A few centers serve as central umbrella agencies for all activities and services relating to older people. They serve also as recruiting spots for volunteers offering opportunities to older people to serve others less active. Some people believe that in time the senior center may come to hold a place in the older person's life equivalent to the central role now played by the school in the lives of children.

Poor nutrition can be caused in part by isolation and loneliness which make it seem hardly worthwhile preparing the food to eat alone. Good nutrition however, provided in a group setting can offer a partial solution to loneliness. Throughout much of life, eating is a social occasion, a time for family gatherings and meetings with friends, birthday parties, holiday picnics all are associated with pleasant times and food. When the social element is removed entirely, many people abandon regular meal times and turn to sporatic snacks to satisfy their hunger. The benefit of eating in a social setting is so important for the mental as well as the physical well-being of older people regardless of income that many organizations are providing group meals in a variety of settings.

Many older people who live alone fear that they may have a fall or be taken suddenly ill and be unable to call for help. Telephone reassurance provides a daily telephone contact for an older person who might otherwise have no outside contact for long periods of time. Persons receiving telephone reassurance are called at a pre-determined time each day. If the person does not answer, help is immediately sent to his home. Usually in the event of no answer a neighbor, relative or nearby police or fire station is asked to make a personal check. Such details are worked out when a person begins receiving this service.

Friendly visiting has been called organized neighborliness because in this kind of program volunteers visit isolated home-bound older persons on a regular schedule once or more often a week. They do such things as play chess and cards, write letters, provide an arm to lean on during a shopping trip or just sit and chat. The essential element is to provide continuing companionship for an elderly person who has no relative or friend able to do so. This kind of visiting relieves loneliness of older people in a very real way. Older people themselves say such things as, "She has made my life over" ... "It makes me feel like I am still somebody worth talking to" ... "It gives me a chance to speak of things which are in my heart" ... "Her visit is something to look forward to." Professional staff workers have observed that clients look better and take more interest in things outside themselves after receiving friendly visiting services. Frequently there is improvement in actual physical condition or at least less absorption in illness.

Living in their own homes is a great desire of many older people. Home services can help make this possible. Some older persons with chronic conditions need regular continuing help preparing meals, keeping the house tidy and personal grooming.

For others help is needed only temporarily while they recover from an illness or while the person who usually gives care is unable to do so. Many older persons may be quite able to handle normal household tasks but need help with heavier chores such as washing walls, moving furniture, cleaning gutters, and taking down storm windows. Accidents which permanently disable people often occur because homes lack minor necessary repair. These in-home services which are available for older people include such things as homemaker service, home health aids, and other similar programs.

Now, what can the counselor do in working with the older American? First, the counselor or psychologist needs not modify his approach for the older client. As with other clients counseling should be a sequentially developed or graduated program providing positive concrete feedback relative to progress and should require not only tasks for the older American but should include a program of graduated decision-making responsibility. Most of us in counseling fail to recognize the need for work adjustment for the older worker of average intelligence with a work history. We feel he can just go back to work if he desires. In our approach to the practice of rehabilitation psychology, adjustment training is for the client with just the opposite qualities — young, mentally retarded and no work history — but the purpose for the work adjustment training is the same in both instances, that is the establishment of an appropriate psychological set. With the young retardate we are trying to establish the self-concept of a worker. With the older worker we are attempting to reestablish this concept.

There are many indications that the majority of the patients on wards in psychiatric institutions are not in need of psychotherapy as much as they need a redefinition of their role in society. A counseling strategy in working with the older American should be one which reverses the isolationism process of aging and one which is designed to add meaning to the lives of each individual older client as well as activities. A counseling program should also take into consideration the need for remotivation of the older American, the gaining of positive feedback of his capability and adequacy and the introduction of the individual to programs which will facilitate the client's psychological adjustment to aging. There are many activities which need mature individuals. These may be activities which are remuniative for the older American or they may be voluntary activities. There is a severe need in our country today for volunteers to help with the less fortunate and the less self-sufficient (Hardy and Cull, 1973; Cull and Hardy, 1974).

REFERENCES

Cull, J. G.: Age as a factor in achieving conformity behavior. *Industrial Gerontology*, Spring, 1970.

Cull, J. G. and Hardy, R. E.: *Volunteerism: An Emerging Profession*, Springfield, Illinois, Thomas, 1974.

Galton, F.: *Hereditary Genius*. New York, 1891.

Hardy, R. E. and Cull, J. G.: *Applied Volunteerism in Community Development*, Springfield, Illinois, Thomas, 1973.

Let's End Isolation, U. S. Department of Health, Education and Welfare, Washington, D. C., DHEW Pub. #(SRS) 73-20129, 1973.

Lorge, I.: Intellectual changes during maturity and old age. *Rev. Educ. Res.*, 17, 1947.

Sprague, N.: Industrial gerontology: A definition and a statement of purpose. *Industrial Gerontology*, Spring, 1970.

Vedder, Clyde B.: *Gerontology*, Springfield, Illinois, Thomas, 1963.

Vedder, Clyde B. and Lefkowitz, Annette S.: *Problems of the Aged*. Springfield, Illinois, Thomas, 1965.

CHAPTER 3

OUTREACH: BRINGING SERVICES TO THE ELDERLY SENIOR CENTERS OF METROPOLITAN CHICAGO

INTRODUCTION
THE SENIOR CENTER AND EFFECTIVE SERVICE DELIVERY
THE ROLE OF THE NEIGHBORHOOD WORKER
CONCLUSION: AN ALTERNATIVE TO INSTITUTIONALIZATION

INTRODUCTION

The Elderly ... Lost in the Shuffle

IN this affluent, opportunity-rich country, one growing segment of the population has been dealt a losing hand. America's elderly have somehow been lost in the shuffle of minority groups struggling for equal rights and a decent standard of living. The reasons for this are numerous and complex, but the result is singularly poignant — the crying needs of many aging Americans, whose productive years have gone to making their country great, are not being met. Aggravating the situation and presaging grave problems for the future, is the fact that the number of elderly is increasing at nearly twice the rate of the general population (1).

Needed . . . A New Approach

Although public and private concern about the plight of the aged has accelerated in recent years, constructive remedial action has been slow in coming. Legislation lags. Social services remain

---

1. McCarthy, Colman, "Politics and Helping the Aging," *The Washington Post,* July 29, 1971, editorial page.

fragmented, and social workers persist in assigning the elderly a low priority. Many senior centers cater to the "well" aged, serving those fortunate few able to attend center functions and often failing to look beyond their walls to the ill, impoverished, and isolated — the so-called "invisible elderly." We have reached a point where the rhetoric of concern and piecemeal action are no longer acceptable. Critically needed is a new approach — a realistic approach, geared to the multiple problems of aging and to delivering tangible, essential services NOW to all aging Americans in need of help, wherever they may be.

An Early Start in Chicago

In the mid-1960's, Hull House of Chicago began exploring ways to reach out to the community elderly. This role was altogether appropriate for Hull House with its settlement house tradition and long history of active involvement with the problems of local neighborhood residents, young and old. A small-scale outreach program was initiated in the Uptown area of Chicago's north side where census figures and personal observation indicated an extremely high concentration of elderly people. Many of the aged there were ill, malnourished, alone, and barely able to make ends meet. Many were utterly confused by the myriad public and private welfare agencies confronting them or were completely unaware that sources of help existed. It was these people that Hull House particularly wanted to reach and serve, by placing the highest priority on outreach into the community and on rehabilitation through services and activities provided by neighborhood senior centers.

The tremendous and immediate human needs revealed by this pilot program in Uptown, and the equally serious plight of the elderly in the adjoining neighborhood of Lakeview, prompted Hull House social planners to begin searching for ways to expand outreach services. This search was ended with the acceptance by the Ililnois State Council on Aging of a proposal for a demonstration project in outreach to the elderly, submitted under provisions of the Older Americans Act. With the authorization of government funds in March 1967, the Lakeview-Uptown Senior

Citizens Project officially came into being. Experimenting with new but basically simple techniques and concepts — most importantly the use of neighborhood workers — the Project staff succeeded in implementing a system for effective delivery of individualized services to the aged on a neighborhood level.

Readily usable written material on how to set up and sustain a program of outreach to senior citizens is, at this point, a scarce commodity. In the following pages, members of the Lakeview-Uptown Project staff have outlined some of their methods and experiences in the hope that these may be of use to others engaged in the important work of helping aging Americans.

THE SENIOR CENTER AND
EFFECTIVE SERVICE DELIVERY

A Central Resource for the Elderly

The priorities of the Lakeview-Uptown Senior Citizens Project have been clear from its inception: to reach out to the invisible neighborhood elderly and to provide them with services to meet their needs. In approaching these objectives, Hull House planners recognized that the needs of the aged are frequently multiple, desperate, and immediate. They envisioned the establishment of a central neighborhood resource equipped to sort out the innumerable social service agencies that the elderly individual encounters, to act as his broker and advocate, to interpret his needs, and to provide or arrange for the appropriate service as quickly as possible. The multi-purpose neighborhood senior center seemed uniquely suited for this task.

In March 1967, two such senior centers were established, one in Lakeview and another in Uptown. These centers provided a congenial place where older people could casually drop in, gather to socialize, engage in recreational activity, or just get away from dreary home environments. But they were service-oriented facilities as well — bases of operation for neighborhood outreach workers and for a small professionally-trained back-up staff.

A Model for Effective Service Delivery

As these centers began serving the community and gaining experience, it became clear that a workable system for maximizing the delivery of available services to the elderly could be achieved on the neighborhood level. The successful functioning of this system depended on coordination of three essential types of services — those of neighborhood/outreach workers, center professional personnel, and related community agencies. By combining its own services and those of other vital programs and organizations into an integrated whole, the center could cope with the multi-problem situations presented by the aging person and not only provide him with services to meet current needs but also help him formulate an overall plan for future years.

Neighborhood Worker Services: The senior center was the axis of the service delivery system. From the center, neighborhood workers moved out into the community, finding isolated elderly, forming friendships, regularly helping the aged with personal tasks, and referring to the center professionals those problems requiring their attention. The neighborhood workers became the center's link with the people of the community, informing local residents about center activities and services, and feeding back information about the neighborhood into the center. Perhaps most important, they provided the tangible supportive services as well as the personal interest and concern which helped make it possible for many homebound elderly to continue living independently.

Center Professional Services: Backing up the neighborhood workers were in-center personnel from a variety of professional disciplines — a social worker, a public health nurse, and a recreation worker. These staff members contributed not only substantive knowledge and direct services in their respective fields, but also know-how in dealing with the many related community organizations and programs. They provided the center's link with outside resources from which aged clients might need assistance. A basic social casework procedure was the professionals' rule of thumb: establish contact with the client, develop an assessment/diagnosis to identify the problem, and formulate a service intervention plan. A strong effort was made to maintain flexibility so that the client's needs would not be lost sight of in a rigid, institutionalized plan of action.

Related Outside Resources: A broad spectrum of outside resources was tapped by the Project's professional workers for the benefit of their elderly clients. The advocacy skills of the workers were regularly used in dealing with such agencies as the Chicago Housing Authority, local Social Security offices, and the Cook County Department of Public Aid. Ongoing relationships with nursing homes, hospitals, and clinics were maintained. Perhaps most interesting and productive, however, was the use of two other Hull House-sponsored programs, specifically designed — like outreach — to provide tangible supportive services for disabled, homebound elderly. The first program, Home Delivered Meals (2), supplied an essential service for physically handicapped older people who might not otherwise have gotten the proper food or perhaps might not have eaten at all. The second, the "Get Together Bus (3)," met another vital need by providing special, free transportation for the aged. The bus was regularly used to distribute Home Delivered Meals and also to transport elderly people to clinics, shopping, and occcasionally on pleasure outings. The Lakeview-Uptown Project successfully coordinated its outreach effort with the Meals and Bus services, thereby enhancing the effects of all three programs. Consequently, it has been possible to provide an integrated and quite comprehensive service which has allowed many elderly people to remain in their own homes and to avoid a dreaded alternative — institutionalization (4).

The successful functioning of the service delivery system is best illustrated through a case example such as that which follows:

2. Originally a demonstration project, funded in part by the U.S. Public Health Service and the Department of Health, Education and Welfare; when the government grant terminated on July 31, 1968, Hull House continued the service with private funds.

3. A government-funded demonstration project administered by Hull House Association under Title III, Older Americans Act.

4. Connolly, Jane F., Director, Senior Centers of Metropolitan Chicago, in testimony in Chicago on November 2, 1971, before the Select Sub-Committee on Education, Committee on Education and Labor, House of Representatives, U.S. Congress.

Mrs. H., a frightened, insecure elderly woman, was discovered by a neighborhood worker who was canvassing a dilapidated building in search of older people who might need help. Mrs. H. was living alone and had completely lost track of her family. After several visits with the worker, Mrs. H. began coming to the Uptown Senior Center for recreational activities. At first she seemed somewhat retarded, but as staff members became better acquainted with her, they realized that she had severe visual and hearing difficulties. Mrs. H. was examined and treated at a clinic, where she was taken by a neighborhood worker. Subsequently, she was admitted to a hospital for cataract surgery, and was fitted with a pair of special glasses. A hearing aid was also secured for her. At about the same time, the Project staff provided another important service by relocating her to better housing. Although her vision and hearing were still impaired, Mrs. H. became more independent, resumed her sewing, and began talking about going back to work. It was as if she had gained a new lease on life because someone cared. Eventually, at the urging of the Project social worker, Mrs. H. decided to return to school; she had dropped out many years earlier at age ten. She entered adult classes at the Urban Progress Center and, in six months of hard work, graduated from the eighth grade. Project staff members — "her family" — attended the graduation and helped Mrs. H. celebrate the happy occasion.

Mrs. H. is planning to continue her education and has enrolled in high school classes. She has literally blossomed and has become an accomplished hostess, frequently entertaining staff and center members in her home. She is still not ready to handle the strains and frustrations of a job, but with social worker guidance and support, Mrs. H. may someday achieve this goal or at least find an acceptable substitute.

The Storefront Center

Over the years, the Lakeview-Uptown Project has had experience with various types of center facilities — facilities within a community center, in a church, in a storefront, and within a senior citizen housing project. Staff and elderly alike agree that by far the most successful has been the storefront center located on a busy street — "where the action is!" The advantages of a storefront are many: it is easily accessible to older people who may be in wheelchairs or have difficulty navigating steps; its large, street-level window is inviting to elderly passers-by; and center participants are able to watch the busy street activity from a secure vantage point but in close enough proximity to feel a part of the community life. The storefront is also beneficial to the outreach effort. This aspect was brought out by a neighborhood worker, who noted,

> The center members loved the storefront, and it was nice for the neighborhood workers too. I felt very comfortable approaching people on the street just outside the center, telling them about our activities and services and then inviting them in. But now that the storefront center is no longer there, I wouldn't *think* of just going up to a strange person on the street like that!

The visible, accessible base of operation afforded by the storefront gave neighborhood workers the confidence and assurance to spread word about the center to local residents, although they were complete strangers, and to actively promote their involvement. The storefront center in Lakeview eventually had to be closed because of inadequate funds. If the needed financial support could be found, the Project staff would strongly favor its restoration.

Senior Center Staff

Facilities are important but people are more so. One of the key factors in the Lakeview-Uptown Project's successful effort has been the cooperative, team approach taken by all staff members. From the outset, center personnel, professional and non-professional alike, joined forces as equals working toward common goals, exhibiting a mutual respect for each individual's contribution to the effort. This situation generated a free and creative exchange of ideas which has greatly facilitated outreach and the delivery of services. The moral support the workers gained from each other was also invaluable. All these factors contributed to the congenial atmoshphere within the senior centers themselves.

The Lakeview-Uptown staff has not been able to do everything the Project's planners suggested in their original proposal. Their priority has been on individual services and in-center activities have accordingly played a subordinate role. The Project might have been strengthened if funds had permitted an expansion of staff, particularly the employment of a trained group worker who could have stimulated and developed more group activities for center members — a vital aspect of rehabilitation for many older people.

THE ROLE OF THE NEIGHBORHOOD WORKER

The Neighborhood Worker . . . "Someone Who Cares"

By far the most interesting, successful and innovative aspect of the Lakeview-Uptown Project has been the use of neighborhood workers. The tangible results produced by these workers, ordinary people with little or no formal training, have astonished Hull House professionals and generated a whole new approach to the field of aging by that agency and its affiliate, Senior Centers of Metropolitan Chicago. The secret of the workers' success seems to lie in the nature and simplicity of the job they perform, a job which utilizes the natural, neighborly impulses of sympathetic people to react as a friend to someone alone or in need of help.

Particularly exciting has been the capacity of the neighborhood workers to fill a vacuum left by generations of professional social workers who have defaulted on service to the elderly. Social workers have traditionally treated the aging like a stepchild (5). For a variety of reasons, they have been unwilling or unable to reach out to or meet the needs of elderly people, increasingly isolated from society by ill health, by loss of friends and loved ones, and by a youth-oriented culture which dismisses them as worthless.

The effects of such isolation, so common among elderly people, are extremely severe. The isolated retreat from reality and become

5. Connolly, Jane F., *Information Center for the Aging: Third Year Report.* Welfare Council of Metropolitan Chicago, Central Services Division, May 1970, p. 31.

withdrawn. They neglect themselves, often eating little or nothing and becoming personally unkempt. They neglect their homes and live in disorder. They lose all sense of time and direction. These people, lonely and in need, remain unreached by social agencies.

Neighborhood workers have been able to fill this gap in services. In a sense, they function as an extension of the caseworker, but their role goes much further. Their unique contribution is in becoming almost a substitute family for aging people who often are homebound and utterly alone in the world. The genuine concern, moral support, and personal friendship which they offer add an entirely new dimension to the traditional social worker-client relationship.

As neighborhood workers make regular visits to the homes of elderly community residents, they personally concern themselves with the well-being of their clients and perform a variety of essential tasks which help the older people meet the normal — but at their age arduous — demands of daily living. These visits give the aging a new stability and direction, a chance to break out of isolation, a base from which to begin relating to the outside world again. Acceptance of help and friendship by the aged often comes slowly; older people are frequently wary of strangers or too proud to accept assistance, and they have been conditioned by sociey o expect rejection. But, as meaingful, trusting relationships develop, the elderly begin sharing their concerns and requesting help, reassurance and advice.

For example,

> A neighborhood worker making visits in a large apartment house rapped on Miss S.'s door. Although there was no reply, there was movement within. The worker identified himself and asked if he could help her in any way. Still there was no reply, so he went away, saying he would return another time. He came back at least once a week, making his presence known by identifying himself. At first, Miss S. only spoke to him through a closed door; eventually she gained enough confidence to admit him to the apartment. Miss S. was neatly dressed and attractive although frightened and suspicious, almost a recluse. The kind of behavior shown toward the worker was typical of her behavior toward her neighbors. Miss S. said she was alone,

ill, and worried about what would become of her. As the weekly
visits progressed, a feeling of trust and faith was established.

At this point, neighborhood workers can try to dispel the
loneliness and insecurity about the future which haunt so many
aging people. At the same time, they can regularly provide
tangible supportive services.

The crucial role of neighborhood workers in this Project
cannot be overemphasized. Their mission of giving the isolated,
despairing elderly a new lease on life is the essence of outreach.

Recruitment of Neighborhood Workers

Outreach work with the aging requires a sensitivity to human
problems, a sympathetic ear, an ability to communicate concern,
a capacity to accept people with all their faults, and an ability to
maintain perspective. Compassionate people in all walks of life
possess these characteristics. In Lakeview and Uptown, a
housewife, a factory worker, a teacher, a small businessman, a
skilled machine operator, and a domestic all became successful
neighborhood workers. These people had in common an inner
strength which enabled them to cope with life's experiences and
command their own lives. All had had positive experiences with
neighborly people. All had a desire to be of service particularly to
the less fortunate, and a genuine liking for elderly people.
Finally, all were in good health. This last characteristic has
proved essential for outreach work because the daily routine is
quite demanding, both physically and emotionally; it involves
not only much walking and stair climbing, but also frequent
exposure to discouraging situations and serious problems.

The Lakeview-Uptown Project has had notable success in
recruiting and utilizing older people from the local communities
as neighborhood workers. As elderly adults themselves, these
individuals shared with their clients a peer-group status which
helped establish rapport. As neighborhood residents, they were
familiar with local shops, community organizations, housing
problems, and so on. And as people with little or no professional
training they were able to deal as equals and as friends with those
they were trying to serve.

No one source provided all of this Project's neighborhood workers. Some have been referred to Hull House by community residents and employment agencies; others have responded to newspaper advertisements; still others have been recruited from senior center memberships. All candidates have been personally interviewed and selected by the Project Director.

Four part-time neighborhood workers were authorized by the grant for the Lakeview-Uptown Project, but Hull House participation in the U. S. Department of Labor's Senior Aide Program has enabled the staff to increase its neighborhood worker component to six people. In addition, the number of workers has periodically been swelled by VISTA and other volunteers. Elderly neighborhood workers and Senior Aides generally work about 15 to 20 hours per week and carry an average weekly case load of twelve clients.

Preparation of Workers for the Job

The process of preparing a new neighborhood worker for the job is a highly informal and individualized one. The elderly workers in Lakeview and Uptown have brought to the job different backgrounds, personalities, and capabilities upon which to build. They have generally been people with insight, a friendly manner, and an ability to competently manage daily affairs. But they have often been somewhat hesitant to take on new social roles in the retirement years. Self-confidence has been carefully instilled and reinforced through a personal relationship with the Project Director and ongoing informal consultation with the reassurance from other staff members. Through this process, the neighborhood workers have developed a definite recognition that their special expertise in communicating with and serving the people of the community is a unique and essential feature of the outreach effort, that their contribution is as vital as that of the professional worker.

Preparation for the job has, in fact, been more an emotional orientation on a one-to-one basis than a formal training procedure. Basic information has been provided gradually so as not to overwhelm the new worker. Little by little, he or she learns the important aspects of public aid and acquires needed information about agencies such as the local housing authority from professional staff members. For the most part, problem situations are dealt with as they arise. When feasible, a new worker is given an opportunity to accompany a more experienced colleague on home visits, a kind of on-the-job training. Soon after, the newcomer is ready to strike out alone, but always with the knowledge and assurance that the professional staff is there to help and provide support — that there will always be someone to come to.

One of the most interesting aspects of this whole process is that the learning experience has been reciprocal. The professional workers have learned at least as much from the neighborhood workers as the latter have learned from the professionals.

The Basic Duties of a Neighborhood Worker

Finding the Elderly: The duties and responsibilities of the neighborhood worker cover a broad range of basic tasks and human services, all of which are important. In the initial stages of this Project, the immediate necessity was for workers to begin locating the elderly who were out there somewhere and in need of help. This search was carried out in a variety of ways, including direct contact with older people in the streets, stores, libraries, laundromats, and nursing homes of the neighborhoods. Door-to-door canvasses were conducted, and isolated elderly were discovered as neighborhood workers talked with landladies, apartment and rooming house managers, tenants and neighbors. Information about the Project's services was given to the public media, to local shops, and to community organizations and churches. The Project's connection with Hull House, long recognized as an agency genuinely dedicated to helping people, brought a positive response from the community. As news of the outreach effort spread, other social welfare agencies began making referrals to the Project staff. The job of finding the invisible elderly was a difficult one which entailed a tremendous amount of aggressive spade work, and it is still going on. Workers continue to find isolated older adults, desperately in need of help but unreached by and even unaware of existing services.

Actual cases, related in the words of neighborhood workers themselves, provide the most vivid descriptions of how the invisible elderly have been located and their needs identified:

> I saw Mrs. H. on the street carrying a heavy shopping bag. Introducing myself as Mrs. A. from Hull House Uptown Center, I offered to help her and walked her to her apartment on the second floor of an ugly, poorly kept building. The stairs were dirty with worn carpeting; the hall was unlit, and the railing pulled out from the wall. Mrs. H.'s two-room apartment was clean but dark, being lit only by single bulbs on the ceiling. Mrs. H. invited me in. She is a pretty woman, 83 years old, who has been a widow for ten years. She walks with a cane. She thanked me for helping her, saying she often feels dizzy on the street, especially when she has to manage both her cane and a shopping bag; still she likes to do her own shopping. I offered to go shopping with her. She seemed anxious to have a friend and someone to call on her. I told her if she would like, I would be able to stop by next Tuesday morning and we could talk about it then.

Providing Tangible Services: Finding an older person and identifying his needs are of little significance unless services can be provided to meet those needs. Again, at this point, the neighborhood workers play a crucial role. They perform some of the most important services themselves. Through "friendly visits" they communicate their concern for the person and establish themselves as friends — "someone who cares." On this basis they are able to offer companionship and moral support, and to ask if there are tangible services they can perform such as shopping for groceries, cashing Social Security checks, writing letters and filling out applications for assistance, picking up medication, taking someone to a clinic — generally doing anything that needs to be done. For instance,

> One of the neighborhood workers in the Lakeview area is able, through friendly visiting and related services, to help a partially blind woman, Mrs. M., remain in the apartment in which she has lived for twenty years. The worker's services include weekly shopping, reading and writing letters. The most interesting service, however, is the worker's assistance in organizing Mrs.

M.'s pantry. Since Mrs. M. can recognize bright colors, a code
has been worked out so that contents of canned goods can be
identified. Canned fruits, for example, have a red label, and are
placed in certain positions on the shelves. This enables Mrs. M
to plan a balanced diet.

Concern about the whole person is a vital aspect of outreach,
and neighborhood workers are visible symbols of this concern,
needed particularly by the lonely, isolated aging. To these people,
especially the physicallly disabled, the outreach services are often
the determining factor in avoiding nursing home confinement.

Telephone Reassurance: Another service handled by the
neighborhood workers themselves involves weekly telephone
reassurance calls to incapacitated oldsters. During one
particularly bad winter when many of the Project's elderly clients
and senior center members were ill or did not venture out because
of the severe weather, the telephone service was expanded.
Neighborhood workers spearheaded the program, but seniors
were also encouraged to regularly call each other. In this way, the
staff was able to dispel some of the loneliness resulting from the
seniors' confinement indoors and to discover if they were getting
the things they needed. The program worked out quite well and
continues for lonely homebound elderly prople with limited
social contact who appreciate occasional telephone conversations
with a friend.

Information and Referral: The needs of many older adults,
however, are not so easily met. Their problems are all too often
multiple and desperate, most frequently concerning health and
finances. Also common are housing difficulties, inaccessibility of
suitable transportation, and exploitation by local merchants and
landlords. The low-income elderly are usually unaware of
existing community resources which can help alleviate their
problems. Here again, the neighborhood worker plays a vital
role, making sure that the aged person knows what services are
available and how to obtain benefits. If a case needs the attention
of a health or social worker, it is the worker's responsibility to
refer it to the center's professional staff.

The Neighborhood Worker and the Professional Worker

Health, recreational and social services have been an integral part of the Lakeview-Uptown Project and its senior centers from the beginning. Although the professionally-trained staff has at times been shorthanded, it has continued to provide services not available elsewhere in the community and to supply constant support for the neighborhood workers. Close cooperation between the latter and the professionals has been essential for the success of the outreach program. With experience, the neighborhood workers have gained an understanding of what kinds of problems they themselves should handle and what should immediately be referred to their professional colleagues. Informal conferences on individual cases are held frequently so that neighborhood workers have continual guidance in handling their clients' difficulties. The professionals provide the expertise in identifying particular health and welfare problems which can be remedied, while the neighborhood workers supply vital information about the community and a unique insight into short and long-term needs of the individual elderly with whom they are personally in touch. Working together, freely exchanging ideas, the staff members devise a comprehensive plan for each client's future years.

The Neighborhood Worker as Enabler and Advocate: In utilizing professional back-up services in specific cases, neighborhood workers act as a bridge between the professional worker or community agency and the client. They may refer a case to a Project staff member or ask the professional to accompany them on a visit to a particular older person's home. The workers may provide moral support for clients by escorting them to the center for counseling or to a referred agency such as the local housing authority. They may even play the advocate role for clients in their dealings with landlords, nursing home licensing authorities, the Department of Public Aid and so on. If the staff arranges for medical treatment or admission to an extended care facility, the neighborhood workers and the professionals follow up the case, visiting the convalescent and working together to see that the client's needs are being met.

When a client can no longer live independently and nursing home or sheltered care placement is the only solution, contact is still maintained through visits. If the home or care facility is still in the neighborhood, the patient is called for and taken to center activities, thus keeping a link with the outside world. Every effort is made to help him feel that he still has a friend and that he is not a forgotten member of society.

The case below, related in the words of the neighborhood worker involved, illustrates well the working relationship between the professional and the neighborhood worker:

> It was a cold day with near zero temperatures and 40 mile-an-hour winds. I was on my way to visit a client when I saw a frail elderly woman waiting to cross the street. A strong gust of wind suddenly knocked her down and her head struck the curb. I went to her assistance and found that her head was bleeding. Several other people had gathered so I asked one of them to stay with the woman while I went into a store to call my supervisor. She advised me to call the police ambulance and to accompany the woman, who was very shaken, to the hospital. I did this and stayed with the woman during emergency treatment and the taking of x-rays. I again called my supervisor and she suggested that I ask the patient if she had a relative or friend whom she would like notified. I then phoned the 80 year old sister with whom the patient lives (she herself being 84) and I waited until the sister arrived. Before leaving, I again called my supervisor to bring her up to date on the case.

> I now visit the two sisters in their home, doing shopping and other errands for them. Because of their advanced age, they may eventually need additional services which I will be able to provide.

The Outreach Goal . . . Rehabilitation and/or Maintenance

In all outreach cases, the objective is to rehabilitate the aging person or at least to enable him to maintain an independent status as long as possible. For many homebound, disabled people, avoidance of institutionalization is the ultimate goal and outreach services are a solution, with arrangements for neighborhood worker services, home delivered meals, and special transportation to clinics via the "Get Together Bus". If these aging people can simply remain in the community in their own homes, their highest hopes will have been realized. When this is no longer possible, the best available institutional care is arranged.

For other older people, the goal may be the regaining of a sense of security throutgh the maximizing of financial resources. In a few cases, this may culminate in part-time employment, but, more frequently, the security will be achieved through application for public assistance, social security, or pension benefits to which the client is entitled.

For still other elderly adults, rehabilitation may be primarily an emotional and a social experience. It may begin with the slow development of a trusting relationship with a neighborhood worker, progress to the regaining of self-confidence, and eventually to active participation in center or perhaps even community activities.

A poignant example of this last type of rehabilitation and the central role played by the neighborhood worker is revealed in the following account:

> In January 1968, a neighborhood worker found Miss S. during a canvass of a community rooming house. Miss S. is single and 65 years old. She has no use of her right arm and wears a brace on her right leg a result of a paralytic stroke. She lives on the third floor and has little communication with the outside world since she cannot afford a phone and the buzzer system of the house phone does not work. Miss S. was very lonely and asked the neighborhood worker, a man, for a "female visitor." This was arranged and after several visits, Miss S. came to the center to discuss some of her problems with the social worker. She stayed to visit with the members present. We have helped her file applications for public housing for the elderly and for food stamps. Miss S. has since joined the cards and gab games activity group, and she was recently observed making a collage with her left hand in an arts and crafts session.

Outreach Work is Therapeutic

In a very special way, some of the neighborhood workers themselves may be the Project's best example of successful rehabilitation through outreach. By participating in the program, elderly workers have broadened their social contacts and fulfilled their personal need to continue helping others. Their salaries also have given them an increased sense of independence. These therapeutic benefits are illustrated in the case of a widower, 66 years old, who joined the staff in March 1969. He noted,

> I like this job. Before I began working, I kept to myself so much I was forgetting how to talk. This job is good for me because it makes me get out and meet people. Now I'm learning how to converse again.

In his capacity as neighborhood worker, this man was exposed to conditions he never knew existed among the very poor. He developed not only a sensitivity to the problems of others, but also an earnest desire to help alleviate them. A man of action, he succeeded in getting an entire apartment building cleaned, painted and fumigated, thereby improving the living conditions of many elderly residents.

Problems Neighborhood Workers May Encounter

Exploitation: In the course of their daily rounds, neighborhood workers encounter a number of difficulties. Their relationships with elderly clients do not always develop harmoniously. Occasionally, older people who are physically able to care for their own needs take advantage of a worker's willingness to help, making unreasonable demands or treating the worker like a servant. Workers must be prepared for potential difficulties of this kind and are cautioned against letting themselves be exploited. Allowing such situations to continue is unfair to workers and does not serve the purpose of outreach — to rehabilitate the elderly and help them help themselves.

The professional can be very supportive in this situation. He can clarify many issues such as why the visit is being made, what tasks should or should not be done by the worker, how much time can be spent with the client, and so on. This provides the worker with a frame of reference and also lets the client know what he can expect.

Overinvolvement: Another danger for neighborhood workers

lies in overinvolvement. Particularly at first, a worker may become too deeply and personally entangled in an older person's problems. Loss of perspective and objectivity often follows, hampering the worker's effectiveness and preventing the identification of specific needs which can be met.

Overwhelming Situations: In still other instances, workers may become overwhelmed by the sheer number and extent of the problems they find; they may feel at a loss as to how to proceed. In such cases, they must realize that their professional colleagues, who are trained to deal with complex situations, can shoulder the burden of finding solutions. In addition, the professionals must make the neighborhood workers aware of the fact that not all problems can be solved; this is sometimes a very difficult idea to accept. The value of always having a professional worker available to talk over such situations as they arise is clear. Regularly scheduled staff meetings and individual conferences are also useful in putting all of these problems into perspective.

A Day with a Neighborhood Worker

A glance at the typical day of a neighborhood worker may be useful at this point. Our worker — we will call her Mrs. C. — begins the morning by telephoning the people she regularly sees on that day to make sure that they want her to drop by as usual. This reminds her elderly friends about the visit, in case they may have absent-mindedly forgotten, and gives the worker a chance to offer to do errands on the way. Mrs. C. also calls and schedules an afternoon appointment with an elderly woman whom a local grocer has noticed in his store and who, he is sure, is nearly blind and in need of help. The grocer knows of Mrs. C. and her work because she often shops in his store for her elderly clients.

Mrs. C.'s first visit is with Miss M. who is 85 years old and confined to a wheelchair. Mrs. C. stops en route to buy a few supplies for her at the drug store. Miss M. cheerfully welcomes our worker and they chat for a while. Mrs. C. inquires about how the home-delivered meals are working out and is assured that the arrangement is very satisfactory. Then Mrs. C. takes Miss M. for their accustomed short outing.

Next on her schedule is a "friendly visit" with Mrs. S., a 65-year-old widow who, because of a heart condition, gets out very little and simply likes to have Mrs. C. come so that she can chat with a friend, serve her coffee, and dress up for an occasion. On this particular day, Mrs. S. has no errands she needs to have done; as always, she comments on how much she looks forward to the visits. She tells Mrs. C., "You're the only one I can always count on." Mrs. C. next stops in briefly to check on Mr. R., who is bedridden, and his elderly wife who cares for him. She brings them a few needed groceries and asks if there is anything Mr. R. needs to make him more comfortable. During the visit, Mrs. R. mentions an elderly neighbor who needs help in finding less expensive housing. Mrs. C. agrees to call the man and offer help.

After lunch at the senior center, Mrs. C. walks to the home of Miss L., the woman referred to her by the grocer. She finds that Miss L. is existing in near isolation in a tiny third floor walk-up apartment, located in a shabby, neglected building. Miss L. seems quite confused and disoriented; she cannot remember when she last had a visitor. After talking with Miss L. a few minutes and discussing her physical and financial troubles, Mrs. C. learns that Miss L., who is 70 years old, thinks she has cataracts in both eyes. She has difficulty doing even the simplest chores because of her poor vision; but she has no money to consult a doctor. Mrs. C. promises to have the staff health worker see about an examination for Miss L. at the eye clinic. The woman also is unaware that she is eligible for Old Age Assistance, and our neighborhood worker offers to help her apply for these benefits. As Mrs. C. is about to leave, the woman thanks her profusely and politely asks her to please come again, "just to visit." Mrs. C. assures her she will come next week and asks if she can run any errands or do any shopping for Miss L. today. Mrs. C. also resolves that during the second visit, she will offer to help clean up the apartment a little; Miss L. cannot see to clean properly and is especially distressed about the condition of the kitchen.

Mrs. C. spends the next half hour visiting residents of a nearby nursing home; some are people she has seen before and some are new acquaintances. They all express appreciation for her visit and for the magazines she has brought, and they ask her to come again. Several mention a desire to attend functions at the senior center if the "Get Together Bus" can pick them up.

Mrs. C. returns to the senior center where she jots down notes about her day's experiences and talks briefly with the health and social workers about Miss L. whose medical and financial problems need professional attention. Then she calls the man whom Mrs. R. had mentioned was in need of housing; Mrs. C. makes an appointment to see him the following day.

Outreach Work is Creative

The Project staff and Hull House have learned a great deal from the neighborhood worker program. First, they have become convinced of the employability of older people and have joined the growing ranks of those demanding that job opportunities be made available to the many elderly who want to continue using their skills and talents in paid or volunteer capacities after retirement. America cannot afford to let this rich resource remain untapped!

Second, neighborhood workers have produced important changes within Hull House itself. In 1968, Senior Centers of Metropolitan Chicago (SCMC), an organization exclusively serving the elderly, entered into an affiliation with Hull House. The Lakeview-Uptown Project became part of SCMC, gaining an advocate and enhanced status within Hull House. Although SCMC support was an important factor in the Project's success, a more interesting development has been the part that neighborhood workers have played in affecting SCMC. The workers' impressive efforts have strongly influenced the thinking of the Board of Directors of SCMC which is now fully committed to the outreach approach for all Hull House senior citizens' programs in Chicago.

CONCLUSION: AN ALTERNATIVE
TO INSTITUTIONALIZATION

The staff of the Lakeview-Uptown Senior Citizens Project considers the successful development of the role of the neighborhood worker its most creative and useful contribution to the field of aging. With advancing years, many people begin to harbor fears that they will eventually be "put away" when they can no longer care for their own needs. This is a particularly strong fear among those Americans with meager financial resources and few family ties. Most people want, above all else, to live out their lives independently in their own homes and communities. Outreach through neighborhood workers can make this hope a reality for many by providing an alternative to institutionalization.

The value of and need for such an alternative are increasingly evident. Nursing home care is frequently unavailable or exorbitantly expensive. Even worse, patients in many care facilities are exploited and brutalized by staff members. Neighborhood worker and related outreach services provide a striking contrast. They are inexpensive, individualized, and humane. They facilitate independent living. They provide social contact — a link with the rest of society — instead of limiting the world of the elderly person to other sick and aged people. In another vein, outreach also is a vehicle enabling more fortunate older people, those who become neighborhood workers themselves, to develop new social roles after retirement.

With life expectancy increasing and the elderly population growing rapidly, the development of new ways to meet the needs of the aging is absolutely essential. Outreach to the elderly through neighborhood workers is an idea whose time has come. Its simplicity makes it a technique adaptable to almost any kind of community, even one with very limited resources. Although the Lakeview-Uptown Project has primarily utilized paid workers and older adults, outreach work can be carried out just as successfully by volunteers and young people under the proper professional supervision. No age or economic group has a monopoly on friendliness or the capacity to help people in trouble.

The relatively small amount of money required to initiate and sustain this sort of operation is, indeed, a wise investment. It is an investment which will begin to indicate its worth almost immediately and will continue to provide dividends for many years to come.

CHAPTER 4

THE AGING WORKER: INSIGHTS INTO THE MASSACHUSSETTS PROBLEM

JAMES L. STEWART

OLDER WORKER PROGRAM OVERVIEW

Introduction

THE daily malaise of the older American is often reflected in reduced income, ill health, physical and mental handicaps, difficult living arrangements, loss of family and friends, loneliness and lack of meaningful activities.

Numerous training and demonstration programs have been implemented to tap the potential and resources of the unemployed and underemployed older worker and to forestall future employment handicaps. Yet, with an increasing population, keener competition and the knowledge demanded by advances in technology and automation, growing numbers of individuals fill the lines of the unemployed; countless individuals work in jobs which do not give full potential to their talents, interests and abilities.

The issue of merely finding a job is no longer the single, nor indeed the basic, criterion for any manpower program. Health conditions or medical disability, lack of education, erratic work history, inadequate skill preparation and experience, legal problems and family pressures often prohibit effective and satisfactory employment.

Perhaps the most illusive barrier to manpower development and programs of solution is societal myth — that the older person is not capable of performing tasks that the younger members of the labor market can.

The late President Kennedy once observed, "The great enemy of truth is very often not the lie — deliberate, contrived and dishonest — but the myth — persistent, persuasive, and unrealistic."

Shrouded in myth, the handmaiden of prejudice, the disadvantaged aging represents not just the loss of manpower, but a loss of wisdom and experience that affects the economy, the family, and general societal enrichment.

Suffering the housing plights of urban areas, job rejection and unemployment, and discontinuous and inadequate health care, he stands alone amidst the current urban revolution as but a member of the "silent multitude." Incapable of mounting effective social protest, this "silent multitude" represents a rapidly growing national constituency most generally unnoticed, unheard, untended and often unwanted.

With only a slight exercise of imagination the full force of the problem hits home when one considers that today the older American represents two-fifths of America's labor force.

In most general terms, the causes for unemployment among older workers have been automation, age discrimination, mergers or plant closings, physical and mental competition with younger employees and unwillingness to retrain for new jobs. But, whether it be because of health or changing patterns or employment opportunities, the tragic fact is that these men and women are jobless, and growing jobless in ever increasing numbers.

In Massachusetts, over 50 percent of the jobless men and women receiving unemployment benefits are over 45 years of age, and their chances of getting another job diminishes every day. Less than 20 percent of those unemployed will find a job through state agencies. And less than nine percent will find employment through private employment agencies.

Results of this extended unemployment problem of older workers in Massachusetts will cause reduced Social Security pension benefits upon retirement — thus creating additional future problems for the worker, economy, and society.

Moreover, the older worker unemployment situation will continue to exist in Massachusetts even though classified ads are filled with appeals by business for help. This condition has existed month after month for the past two years in the greatest economic boom in Massachusetts history.

This state of labor supply and demand has also had an important influence on employer hiring policies in the past two years. Restrictions such as pension, insurance, and health plans, forced retirement, and age have been relaxed or overlooked in skilled, semi-skilled, clerical, manufacturing industry, semi-professional and with the traditionally lower paid retail sales and services.

In addition to the aforementioned market conditions, the older worker has an unreal and misplaced understanding of and belief in what his capabilities are and the potential he believes needs development. Thus, a Gordian Knot has occured in which the employer, while in need of manpower, cannot and does not want to see what the older worker has to offer and the older worker, while in economic and general environmental distress, offers more than he is capable of delivering. Even if there is an older worker willing to accept a demotion in terms of salary, position and responsibility, the employer will select a younger person instead of a qualified older worker.

Measurable Orientation

The John F. Kennedy Family Service Center, Inc., under two contracts with the United States Department of Labor, has devoted the better part of three years in the study of the problems of older workers as part of a seven-city demonstration project of the U. S. Department of Labor. Gainful employment has been found for 983 individuals out of 1,119 applicants, but in comparison to the level of unemployment in the Commonwealth of Massachusetts, the job ahead is still unchallenged.

The success of the Kennedy Center's Older Worker Program must be attributed in large measure to the multi-service context which provided complementary service in family counseling, mental health consultation, recreation, legal assistance, and general social service. The unemployed older worker is not simply regarded as a placement problem. The Center is concerned with all the elements of his life that could possibly militate against his satisfactory reemployment.

Cost Benefit Analysis

One measure of the "success" of the Older Worker Program is the ratio of the benefits both qualitative and quantitative to the participants of the program to the costs of the program.

Qualitative benefits include increased confidence, increased ability to cope with the environment, and general improvement in the "quality" of life. The quantitative benefits are simply the increments to income that resulted from participation in the program. If the sum of the benefits of the program exceeds the costs, then the program has justified its existence in terms of its contribution to the social and economic well-being of the populace.

The increased motivation and confidence of an unemployed older worker, who has been placed in a suitable job by the Older Worker Program, is clear to his friends and family but impossible to measure or quantify in any meaningful fashion. Only the quantitative benefits of the program can be measured in the benefit-cost ratio. It is important to bear in mind that this ratio underestimates the "true" value of the program, for it does not include the general improvement in the 'quality" of life of the applicants.

To implement the measurement of the benefit-cost ratio, the following methodology was utilized.

The entire population was stratified into three groups: directly placed, indirectly placed, and case closed as of the end of the contract. The direct and indirect placement groups were still employed as of July 31, 1968, while the case closed group included applicants who had been placed during the contract period.

A random sample of 16 percent of the population in each stratum was made to obtain the following data:

Income before placement

Income after placement

Length of employment

The sample data were calculated to yield the following information for each stratum:

Average monthly income before placement

Average monthly income after placement

Average tenure on the job

The sample results were then expanded to the entire population. (See Formula A, Appendix I, for calculations relevant to Table I and following statement.)

TABLE 1

Status as of July 31, 1968	Number in Population	Number in Sample	Average Monthly Income Before Placement	Average Monthly Income After Placement	Average Length of Time on the Job (Months)
Direct Placement	84	10	$108	$358	11.4
Indirect Placement	183	29	$84	$393	15.2
Case Closed	327	60	$67	$212	5.0
TOTAL:	594	99			

The benefits of the program exceed the costs by 344 percent. In addition, this measure only indicated the *yearly* level of benefits to the recipients, and not the *lifetime* earning increases to the recipient. Thus, the benefit-cost ratio is underestimated; for many of the applicants will continue to maintain their present level of income for the remainder of their working lives.

For example, if it is assumed that, on the average, ten percent of each stratum will maintain their jobs for five years at the average monthly income predominative for that stratum, the additional benefit-cost can be calculated via the Formula B in Appendix I.

Thus, even after the very conservative hypothesis of a job retention rate of only ten percent, the Kennedy Center's Older Worker Program has a benefit-cost ratio of 4.38; that is, the benefits of the program exceed its costs by 438 percent.

If the most optimistic assumption were made of 100 percent retention, the benefit-cost ratio would be 43.8; that is a return of 4380 percent for every dollar spent on the program.

Of course, the methodology utilized in these calculations is only a rough approximation of the true benefits of the program. However, the calculations do verify the fact that the Kennedy Center's Older Worker Program has "succeeded" to a large extent in fulfilling the needs of its applicants.

Program Focus

Within the framework of the multi-service center and guided by realistic goals and a substantial program format, the Older Worker Program has been able to deliver employment services, while bringing to bear family counseling, legal assistance, mental health consultation, recreation, social services, and other welfare services to the total resolution of individual problems.

The Kennedy Center, through the Older Worker Program, offered employment services to:
— those who were unemployed;
— those who were not working at their highest level of skill;
— those who were handicapped by lack of job training or experience or have no marketable skill; and,
— those whose educational preparation, work attitudes or personal problems made maintenance of steady employment difficult.

The goals of the Older Worker Program were designed to:
— locate, identify, and attempt to activate adults (45 years and older) toward reemployment;
— direct those older workers, whenever necessary, to work preparation, training, and retraining which will enable them to reenter full-time employment;

— place older workers in permanent jobs commensurate with their abilities and skills;
— open up new jobs to older workers by taking advantage of new training and employment opportunities that can be developed directly or indirectly from Boston's diversified labor market;
— demonstrate multi-service center concept can improve the older worker employability by providing psychological counseling and health and welfare services;
— provide counseling and employment services to persons over 62 who may be on Social Security or pension and seek to supplement family income on a part-time basis without jeopardizing retirement benefits; and,
— demonstrate the effectiveness of innovative group techniques in increasing the employability of white-collar unemployed older workers by organizing them into an effective self-help job development and placement organization.

The Older Worker staff has been able to:
— deal with personal and family problems affecting employability;
— evaluate the work capabilities and potential of the older worker;
— counsel and place the older worker into gainful employment;
— investigate the real and imagined employment barriers to hiring the older worker;
— deal with and ameliorate personal and emotional problems evidenced by "hard core" applicants; and,
— recommend solutions in placing the older worker into gainful employment.

In the course of delivering employment and counseling services, the Older Worker Program practiced a two-dimensional approach to the unemployed older worker:
— within the traditional framework, provision of MDTA, basic education programs, adult education and job placement programs; and,
— within the restructured framework to deal with the "hard core" applicant, one who does not fit into the traditional labor market due to the severity or chronicity of his problems.

Age, lack of education, training, skill, experience, ability to adjust, lack of confidence, lack of knowledge of reentry into labor market are the usual marketable dimensions which the employer and older worker believe are the older worker's barriers to effective job placement and performance.

Yet the Older Worker Program's three years of experience have uncovered the roots of these dimensions as delineated by the following "hard core" characteristics:
— alcoholism;
— physical disability;
— mental disability;
— emotional problems; and,
— questionable employability age (over 72, physically unable to work), language barrier, unmotivated, unrealistic restrictions regarding hours, salary and location, police record, poor work history, lack of experience, unstable work history.

The Older Worker Program has determined that 310 or 48.44 percent of its 640 registered applicants and 26 out of 32 or 81.25 percent of the unregistered applicants fall within one or more of these "hard core" categories.

The remaining 330 or 51.56 percent of the applicants to the Older Worker Program are categorized as regular applicants with age, skill level, lack of confidence and lack of knowledge of reentry techniques into the labor market being their only barriers to securing employment at every skill level.

The Older Worker

For purposes of exposition, the applicants and enrollees to the Older Worker Program have been categorized as comparison and target groups. The target group represents a selected geographic location within the city of Boston, while comparison refers to all other persons applying to the program.

The typical Older Worker enrollee to the Kennedy Center's Older Worker Program is sixty years old, has had 11.2 years of education, is earning on the average of $75 a month, has been unemployed for twenty-six weeks prior to application, and has held an average of two jobs in his working career.

The skill level data, presented in Table II, indicates that the enrollees in the program have the skills that are most in demand in today's economy; namely, professional-managerial, semi- and skilled labor, and service skills. Twenty-two (22) percent of the enrollees were classified as "unskilled," a sector for which demand is being drastically curtailed. Although most applicants have varying degrees of "hard core" characteristics, as noted in later discussion, these unskilled individuals, having the severest "hard core" problems, evidenced the greatest need for job retraining, counseling and multi-services. Thus, these data indicate that in spite of relatively high education and skill levels the average enrollee has had an unsuccessful employment history.

TABLE II

Skill Level (Total Population N=640)

OCCUPATION	PERCENT PRIMARY OCCUPATION	PERCENT LAST OCCUPATION
Professional Managerial	8.9	7.7
Middle Managerial	9.4	10.8
Clerical and Sales	10.8	10.8
Skilled	5.6	5.0
Semi-Skilled	9.5	8.0
Menial Clerical	16.2	15.0
Service, Protective, Health	3.6	3.6
Service, Food Processing	4.5	4.7
Service, Building	9.5	11.7
Unskilled	22.0	22.7
	100.0%	100.0%

Table III provides a partial explanation for this incongruity; only 52 percent of the enrollees in the program were free from the emotional, mental, physical, and attitudinal problems. "Hard core" characteristcs were determined for 48 percent of the enrollees in spite of high skill and educational levels.

A comparison of the characteristics of the "hard core" and

TABLE III

"Hard Core" Characteristics N=640

Non "hard core"	51.56%
Alcoholic	14.54%
Physical disability	18.58%
Mental disability	1.72%
Emotional disability	5.00%
Questionable employability	8.60%
	100.00%

"non-hard core" recruited by the program reveals that the average "non-hard core" enrollee is sixty years of age, has completed 11.7 years of school, has an average monthly income of $90, has been unemployed for twenty weeks, and has held a job for an average maximum of 14.21 year. While the average "hard core" enrollee is sixty years of age, he has only completed 10.6 years of school, has an average monthly income of $60, has been unemployed for thirty-three weeks, and has held a job for a maximum of 12.6 years.

TABLE IV

Comparison of Skill Levels of "Hard Core" and "Non-Hard Core"

	Percent "Non-Hard Core" N=330	Percent "Hard Core" N=310
Professional Managerial	10.6	7.1
Middle Managerial	11.8	6.8
Clerical and Sales	13.9	7.4
Skilled	5.8	5.5
Semi-Skilled	7.3	11.9
Menial Clerical	19.4	12.6
Service, Protective, Health	3.6	3.5
Service, Food Processing	3.9	5.2
Service, Building	7.3	11.9
Unskilled	16.4	28.1
	100.0%	100.0%

Furthermore, Table IV indicates that there is a significant difference in the primary occupation skill levels of the "hard core" and "non-hard core" population. While 42.1 percent of the "non-hard core" have primary skills in the highly desired professional and managerial, middle managerial, clerical and sales, and skilled levels, only 26.8 percent of the "hard core" possess these primary skills. Similarly, while only 16.4 percent of the "non-hard core" are in the unskilled category, 28.1 percent of the "hard core" are found in this sector.

While there are no significant differences in the mean age and education level of the "hard core" and "non-hard core" population, significant differences occur in that the "hard core" applicants have been unemployed for a longer period of time; have a lower level of income; and have a shorter employment history than the "non-hard core." They also have a lower level of primary skills than the "non-hard core."

A significantly higher incidence of "hard core" characteristics appeared in the target population, i.e., 54 percent of the target group had "hard core" characteristics, as opposed to 46 percent in the comparison group. Moreover, the "average" target enrollee was 57 years old, completed 9.7 years of education, earned an average of $55 a month, had been unemployed for twenty-eight weeks before entering the program, and had been employed for an average of 10.3 years in his working career. The average comparison enrollee, on the other hand, was 60.5 years old, completed 11.9 years of education, had an average monthly income of $80 a month, had been unemployed for an average of twenty-four weeks, and had been employed for an average of 14.84 years. The average target enrollee is less educated, more disadvantaged, and has a less stable work history than his counterpart. As indicated in Table V, there is a vast difference in the primary skill levels. Only nine percent of the target group had skills in the professional managerial, middle managerial, clerical and sales, and skilled levels, while 46.2 percent of the comparison group had skills in these desirable occupations.

Particular "hard core" problems (see Table VI) were evidenced in the target group, viz., a severe incidence of alcoholism and a significantly higher level of attitudinal factors, placing them in the "questionable employment" sector.

TABLE V

Skill Level — Primary

	TARGET	IOMPARISON
	%	%
Professional Managerial	0.5	12.7
Middle Managerial	2.0	12.7
Clerical and Sales	2.5	14.5
Skilled	4.0	6.3
Semi-Skilled	6.0	11.2
Menial Clerical	16.2	16.2
Service, Protective, Health	6.5	2.4
Service, Food Processing	4.5	4.5
Service Building	19.1	5.2
Unskilled	38.7	14.3
	100.0%	100.0%

TABLE VI

Percent of Distribution of "Hard Core" Characteristics

	N=199	N=441
	%	%
Alcoholic	19.6	12.3
Physical Disability	20.1	18.0
Mental Disability	2.0	1.6
Emotional Disability	4.0	5.4
Questionable Employment	8.0	8.8
Total "Hard Core"	53.7	46.1
Total "Non-Hard Core"	46.3	53.9
Total Population	100.0%	100.0%

To summarize, of the 640 enrollees, 330 were "non-hard core" and 310 had "hard core" characteristics. Similarly, out of the 640 enrollees, 199 were from the target group and 441 were from the comparison group. The incidence of "hard core" characteristics was, generally, significantly higher in the target group. Furthermore, there was a severely high incidence of alcoholism among the target group. On the average, the "hard core" enrollees had a poorer work history and were more disadvantaged than the "non-hard core" enrollees, despite the fact that both groups of enrollees had strikingly high levels of education.

RECOMMENDATIONS

With the body of this document describing the completed Older Worker Program in its particular functional parts, these recommendations emphasize that the problems besetting the older worker are not solved, and that no one approach will suffice in the solution. However, based on experience, certain elements must appear in any program or approach in order to deal comprehensively with the older worker; earlier program intervention must address itself to those as young as 21 years of age; and provision must be made for those who will never be able to enter a competitive labor market, yet who want to and can still make some productive contribution in a therapeutic environment.

A general statement representing generic elements applicable to any older worker program will be followed with specific service, program and/or setting recommendations which taken separately or coordinated into an inner city, state or regional manpower framework would serve to begin the difficult task of replacing the older and aging worker into American society.

Past experience in manpower programs has demonstrated the distinct advantage of a multi-service approach to the satisfactory and gainful employment of this age group. Within the multi-service framework with qualified personnel, the applicant 45 years of age and older needs counseling and placement with a new understanding of program techniques and personnel and revision of the applicant's attitude toward himself, his job role and his abilities. The counseling and placement process includes the resolution of short-term problems and continuous services for long-term difficulties in order to help the older worker adapt and adjust to the competitive labor market.

New counseling techniques (individual and group), new health components (mental and physical), and training facilities, half-way houses, retirement programs provide innovative directions toward the adjustment and personal fulfillment of this applicant.

Identification, assessment, evaluation and rehabilitation of the older worker before placement into gainful employment is a program necessity. Comprehensive health services, including medical, surgical, psychiatric and dental care, need to be available to the older worker applicant.

Individual motivational levels require examination to determine factors which inhibit the older worker from taking advantage of training or employment opportunities. Based on this assessment, such techniques as the use of teaching machines and group therapy need to be utilized and evaluated in their success in motivating the reorienting the older worker to the need for a productive working life.

Retirement counseling for those applicants who find it difficult to adjust to being unemployed needs to be incorporated. Applicants would benefit from intensive counseling regarding available part-time jobs, hobbies and other culture and leisure time services and activities.

Crucial to the effective placement of the older worker is a responsive and accepting attitude on the part of industry. Any program must engage the interest and participation of relevant programs for hiring and retraining the older worker in light of company policy and attitude toward this worker, reflect attitude changes on the part of both the employee and the employer and evaluate the job effectiveness, stability and performance of an older worker in this situation.

General Employment

The older worker has been isolated even in terms of special programs geared to serve his employment needs. Yet the problem of unemployment and underemployment occur in many cases earlier than the artificial age distinction of 45 years of age.

General employment services, beginning with any individual 21 to 44 years of age, who requires training and job placement and more particularly medical and health assessment and counseling with psychiatric or psychological aid, begin the real attempt to forestall the aggravated problems which occur in later life. The outreach aspects of the general employment approach needs considerably more attention and staff effort because these individuals are more difficult to identify; most are not aware of the seriousness of their problems, and they are still young enough to get any kind of job. Certain groups will readily qualify for any program, e.g. those currently employed as casual laborers. Others who are employed full time but are working below their capacities will be more difficult to reach.

Counseling and testing programs would be modified and adapted to take into account the life style and experiential history of the applicants. A greater emphasis would be placed on non-verbal testing and other tests not subject to culture bias. Because of the client's work habits, work experiences and attitudes, the style and tempo of the interviewing procedure and counseling process would take into account the many additional factors which have to be considered and assessed (e.g. feasibility of formal training vs. on-the-job training, advisability of returning to school when balanced against family and home responsibilities).

The placement aspect of an employment program would include intensive follow-up; the most significant variabale is the quality of the placements effected. These services would include those individuals not participating in any of the special employment programs or projects instituted to deal with particular employment problems encountered due to age, physical or mental disability or other relevant personal factors.

Program techniques for upgrading underemployed personnel would involve such training programs as Manpower Development and Training Act, on-the-job training, vocational guidance and counseling, basic education, adult training courses, utilization of scholarships and federal grants and referral to both vocational and academic programs at local universities and vocational schools or private institutions.

Special methods would be utilized for the unemployed "hard core" applicant whose difficulty may be related to a police record, alcoholism, lack of motivation, emotional, mental or physical disabilities. Mental and physical health services, legal assistance, special testing, job development, placement and follow-up would be geared to meet the special difficulties of the "hard core" applicant 21 to 44 years of age as he seeks reentry into the labor market.

The applicant in search of part-time employment, whether a housewife, a student, physically disabled person, or one in the process of recuperation and rehabilitation, would receive vocational training, adult education, and will be encouraged to participate in community activities or an existing sheltered workshop, e.g., Morgan Memorial or PACE Industries in Boston.

The possibility of the use of the computer to assist in the matching of applicants with fluctuating labor market demands might be a fruitful area for investigation. If feasible, this would:
— allow for more systematic study of the characteristics of the match and mismatch process in employment;
— effect the study of gainful employment on other parameters of the life situation, e.g., parent-child relations, marital discord, general health status;
— characterize those companies where employment stability occurs, e.g., size, pension policies, participation in fringe benefits, kind of work, opportunities for advancement, location of company from home; and,
— allow the development of networks of such data banks for regional comparisons and application.

Cooperative Occupational Opportunities Program

The everyday experience of attempting to find suitable and stable employment for individuals with one or more chronic physical and/or emotional difficulty or those able-bodied retirees in need of supplementary income or assistance with retirement adjustments necessitates a community workshop environment to halt their productive loss to the labor market. Such a community workshop would provide employment for those who can work on a full- or part-time basis, at their own pace and according to their own interest and ability in a supportive atmosphere.

This community workshop or a Cooperative Occupational Opportunities Program would include such elements as:

— the provision of employable skills for continued work in the workshop or for outside employment;

— therapeutic assistance (both individual and group) and training to those with limited ability due to alcoholism, mental illness or physical retardation or disability;

— work evaluation in determining motivation for work and type of work applicants are interested in and capable of performing;

— development of work habits and attitudes in a non-threatening situation in order to return those able to gain employment in industry;

— training and retraining applicants who can learn specific marketable skills enabling them to take regular employment or participate in the ownership of one of the "Coop" ventures or participate in any community service program; and,

— extension of full-time or part-time employment within the program on a continued basis at a minimum wage for those who will never be able to return to regular employment.

Follow-up and supportive services such as social services, family counseling, legal aid, psychological and medical care and any other multiple service would assist the "Coop's" staff in the resolution of those problems which in fact necessitated the establishment of this workshop.

Close liaison with local industry and business would permit employer-employee evaluations and better determination of the capabilities and performance of these workers. Local businesses could offer support in subcontracting various jobs, such as general bench assembly work, general office procedures including collating, filing, bookkeeping, typing, mimeographing, etc. Profits from subcontracts would provide supplemental wages insuring a minimum wage for employees. Candy making, candle-making, woodworking, etc., would also provide a source of income when sold by "Coop" owned retail outlet or through business outlets. Cafeteria services, general cafeteria work and related service occupations would be included.

Elderly shut-ins could be offered simple piece work (jobs which would be distributed by "Coop" and assembled in their homes). They could also be encouraged to use leisure time skills, such as knitting, sewing, crotcheting, embroidering, etc., to produce items to be sold by the "Coop" outlet. The proceeds for the sale of these items would provide supplemental income for the shut-ins.

In addition to the economic aspect, the shut-ins will derive self-esteem, a feeling of adequacy, better inter-personal relationships and an increased zeal for living.

Personnel

The best program and approach falls far short of intended goals if qualified and sensitive personnel are not equipped to deal with the complex factors surrounding the employment of the older and aging worker. The economics of the labor market are not merely an issue since the mere fact of age and all its attendant social, physical, and psychological variables affect how one will work and at what one is able to work. A job counselor who understands the labor supplies and demands is not effective, if he does not understand the necessity for social services referral or internment in a half-way house before a job applicant can be sent out to work.

This final document aptly records the number of applicants who were placed and who quickly terminated because they were not identified as "hard core" under the initial program orientation. Based on this telling experience, specific pre- and in-service orientation must be conducted for any and all personnel participating in an older worker program. Moreover, professional staff such as psychiatrists, psychologists, gerontologists, and specialized social work emphasis must be built into programs for the older worker as most of his difficulties in finding and holding employment are related to issues of age.

The contribution the older or aging individual can make in case finding, pre-counseling interviews, follow-up and related administrative tasks in an employment program has yet to be tested.

Neighborhood Adult Corps

A Neighborhood Adult Corps would permit adult work crews to service the community or other non-profit local activities. This Corps would be especially pertinent to the "hard core" unskilled since it would generate renewed interest in productive contribution to the community, provide personal satisfaction through accomplishment and would begin the development of work discipline in a mutually supportive atmosphere under the direction of an indigenous crew leader.

Human Relations Training

Supervisors, foremen and union representatives of small and medium sized companies are important mediators of support, intervention and early case finding in the life of its employees, particularly the older workers. Education through human relations training programs should apprise these personnel of the basic needs and attendant problems of the older worker. Their unique organizational position should permit the effective incorporation not only of employment training programs, but also of social and mental health components for the securing and retraining of competent, healthy older workers.

Older Worker Institute

The Older Worker Institute should constitute a forum of successfully placed and satisfied older workers. It should explore and analyze the factors contributing to change in work motivation and attitudes of the older worker and the impact on and response of the employer to competent, productive older workers. Management, executives and union representatives should be invited to participate as observers, lecturers or as recruitment officials.

Training Program for Engineering, Electronics, Retail and Machine Shop Industries

Through a community multi-service center, such as the

Kennedy Center, or employment program, an ad hoc training program for engineering, electronics, retail and machine shop industries would meet the demands for skilled labor. Those industries in short supply of labor might submit their requests through a central local, state or regional office for such labor. If sufficient interest is evidenced, courses could be devised quickly and economically. Moreover, due to this relationship between an employment agency and industry, the older worker would be guaranteed a job once he has successfully completed the course. This kind of approach would also permit the relocation of able older workers to move to those areas where employment would be guaranteed.

Half-Way House

The creation of a special unit where anyone in a particular community suffering the ill effects of an alcohol drinking experience would permit treatment, observation and rehabilitation. Cooperating community agencies and facilities might be prepared to take on this individual after his stay in the half-way house with environmental adjustment and employment. This facility would not be available for alcoholics alone but for anyone who cared to come or is brought. The unit would be open only in the evening hours for maximum but not complete coverage and would require personnel sufficiently sophisticated medically to know when to send the person with impending delirium tremors or other problems to the local participating hospital.

Local health facilities must be utilized especially since the treatment requires regular visits to a clinic for fairly long periods of time. If the community sees health in action on behalf of the alcoholic patient directly, the "feedback" effects in requesting help sooner and a more helpful treatment prognosis may become the expectation. This unit must be located in the community, otherwise it loses its purpose.

The entire thrust of the alcohol problem approach must rely on early casefinding, prevention and community involvement.

Institute on Industrial Gerontology

An Institute on Industrial Gerontology would constitute an interdisciplinary and broad institutional commitment to applied research and professional training in the field of Industrial Gerontology. This university-based Institute, with participation from industry and community agencies, would begin the necessary task of searching for answers to job redesign, preparatory retirement counseling, health conditions affecting employability, cost factors in pension and insurance plans, production capacities, motivational and attitudinal factors and sensitive personnel and management practices.

ADMINISTRATION

Appropriate reference may be made to the Interim Report and the Older Worker Final Report for specific explanation of staff, administration, procedures and forms.

New approaches or techniques are woven into those sections where they function as part of the program operation rather than isolating them artificially in this section. Of particular note are the new recording forms and procedures developed and expanded to assist the employment counselor in his evaluations. Under the supervision of the Kennedy Center's Associate Director, a clinical psychologist, meetings were held with the counselors. From these a more technical and detailed interviewing and counseling method evolved. The counselors made a concerted effort to relate carefully the employment situation to the applicant's ability and interest.

Two systematic methods provided information concerning the employability and employment stability of the older worker and enhance the compilation of employment data on the older worker. The classification of direct placements included a complete work record of each applicant; a chart with the name of applicant, date of interview, date of placement and name of employer with whom placed and a cross check of this system by recording this information in a central office card file, and the incorporation of simultaneous entries from the vocational counselor's interview sent directly to the central office file.

A *Standard Operating Procedure Manual* provided a set of reference guidelines for the vocational counselors and other staff members in establishing operational procedures for intake, counseling, placement, status, follow-up, classification, referral procedures, record keeping, job listings, and other policies.

A copy of this manual appears in Appendix II.

A consultant is running a logistic regression to predict the probability distribution of a person being placed given certain characteristics such as age, sex, residence, and skill level. The regression will serve the following purpose:

— it will predict which characteristics mitigate against a person being placed; and,

— it will predict which characteristics give the highest probability of placement, thus, the regression will serve as both a predictive and explanatory model. The particular form of the model will, of course, be a function of the "goodness of fit" of the alternate schemes.

RECRUITMENT

The recruitment for the Older Worker Program within the Charlestown area was instituted soon after the opening of the Kennedy Center and continued through the following channels until the program's termination.

All community facilities and personnel were notified. Information regarding the project was given to the Federation of Charlestown Organizations, a fifty-member organization of the district's six churches, together with the social, veteran, business, union, fraternal and service groups.

Announcements were made from the church pulpits, and the church bulletins described the program in full. Placards describing the project's employment services were placed in church lobbies, meeting halls, the public housing project, banks, schools, store fronts and other trafficked locations.

News releases and articles in the local and metropolitan newspapers highlighted the activities of the project. Of particular impact were the person-to-person communications and discussions initiated by the enthusiastic and satisfied applicant.

"Ability Is Ageless" Conference

The Kennedy Center, in cooperation with the U. S. Department of Labor, conducted the ABILITY IS AGELESS Conference at Boston College on June 18, 1968.

Massachusetts Governor John A. Volpe opened the Conference with "It is time that we consider the elderly as a resource rather than a problem." He stated further that "It is apparent that much constructive effort and pioneering activity are going forward at the Kennedy Center in the quest for the improvement of our rapidly changing urban America." As the concluding speaker, Boston Mayor Kevin H. White offered the support of City Hall and said "... we can hope with some sense of optimism to transfer today's rhetoric into realistic employment programs for the workers of tomorrow through programs like the Kennedy Center's."

The participants were prominent businessmen, legislators, union representatives, educators, medical authorities, and state, local and federal government officials.

The day-long Conference enabled the discussion and analysis of the techniques and new avenues of cooperation between major institutions and agencies for improving the employability of the older worker.

The Conference participants responded to the deepening concern that various institutions and agencies have for older workers who seek employment in the face of such obstacles as age, premature forced retirement, limited job opportunities for those over 45, poor health, lack of confidence, or inability to adjust to new work situations and ignorance of the techniques for smooth reentry into a competitive labor market.

As new service systems were explored that would effectively deal with this ever expanding problem, traditional policies, current thinking and program operations and myths regarding the older worker were challenged. With the program keynote that today's public and private agency and institutional programs are insufficiently adaptable to these problems, corollary questions, working solutions and thoughtful observations and conclusions summed up the Conference's probe of today's older worker issues.

Conference publicity brought new applicants to the program as well as interesterd industrial and institutional personnel who were unaware of available older worker programs in the greater Boston area or of those individuals working with the older worker. Moreover, the Conference participants stated that they had an opportunity to hear different viewpoints with regard to the problem of the older worker and to air some concerns in this public forum.

An "Ability Is Ageless" report is currently in production and will be disseminated nationally to further enhance continued discussion and awareness of those working in the interests of the older worker, and of programs and issues relevant to his employment situation.

Unregistered Applicants

During the last eight months of the Older Worker Program, initial interviews were conducted by a psychological counselor. These interviews revealed Older Worker applicants as being in extremely poor physical and mental health prohibiting acceptance for job counseling and placement.

A total of 32 unregistered applicants, 22 or 69 percent male and 10 or 31 percent female, were offered multiple services but did not accept any long-term assistance.

"Hard core" characteristics included, in order of highest occurance, alcoholism, mental disability, physical disability, and emotional disability which represents 75 percent of the unregistered applicants.

Sixteen percent were not interested in any program assistance and 3 percent came to the Center only to become eligible for other benefits such as unemployment compensation.

Questionable employability, e.g., senility and lack of motivation, accounted for six percent of the unregistered applicants. Table VII reveals the reasons given by the applicant for not registering with the Older Worker Program.

Here lies perhaps the most frustrating element of any program

TABLE VII

REASON FOR NOT REGISTERING	NUMBER	PERCENT
Would not comply with social service referral	6	19
Evaluation by social services — unemployable	13	41
Inquiring	2	6
Seeking assistance other than employment	2	6
Comply with DES for unemployment benefits did not want employment	1	3
Advised to return to present position	1	3
Wanted to continue with unemployment benefits	1	3
Awaiting medical evaluation	1	3
Not interested	5	16
TOTAL:	32	100%

geared to finding employment for the older worker since the unregistered applicant will not accept any multiple service to aid in his rehabilitation.

JOB DEVELOPMENT — EMPLOYERS ACCEPTANCE OF THE OLDER WORKER

In the early months of the Older Worker Program, job development was accomplished in part through a direct form letter. During the first six months of the Program over 500 companies received a letter explaining the Older Worker Program and job order requests for qualified older workers.

The response from 255 companies produced 2,355 positions available for qualified older workers. Unfortunately, the distribution of jobs developed was not congruent with the distribution of primary skill levels of the enrollee. For example, while 116 applicants had primary skills in the professional, managerial, and middle management levels, only 20 positions were developed in these skill areas. In addition, many of the applicants who did qualify by skill level were rejected because of age, health, or other "hard core" characteristics.

The follow-up with personnel interviewers generally indicated one of the following reasons for the rejection of skill qualified applicants:

— applicants could not pass a company physical; and,
— positions in which the applicant was qualified for had been filled.

Further investigation by the Older Worker Staff with insurance and banking organizations led to the underlying reasons for skill qualified applicants rejection. Pension, insurance costs, mandatory retirement and company rejection policies were cited as reasons for not hiring Older Worker applicants especially those with "hard core" characteristics. However, one executive stated that because of the tight labor needs in the Greater Boston area many companies were hiring older workers especially in clerical and menial clerical positions. This executive explained that accepted applicants were generally under 60 years of age and did not evidence any "hard core" characteristics.

A study conducted by a local insurance company on recently hired older workers shows:

1. The retention rate for males and females in both clerical and non-clerical positions was three times better with hirees over age 50 than it was for the total company.

2. Absence of both males and females was considerably less for over age 50 than for the companies experience overall.

3. Duration of absence, by males hired for both clerical and non-clerical positions over age 50 was for a shorter term. Females hired for clerical positions experienced a slightly higher duration (ten days vs. nine days per year) than the company average, but those in non-clerical positions provided more favorable experience than the female counterparts in similar type assignments.

This study reinforces the high stability ratio of older workers who were "non-hard core" direct and indirect (1) placements.

Additional studies have shown the productivity of older

---

1. i.e. Kennedy Center placed and "found jobs themselves" respectively.

workers equivalent to that of younger employees.

It was the consensus of the Older Worker staff that job opportunities did not materialize and employer attitudes changed because of such productivity studies.

The Older Worker Program conducted follow-up interviews with personnel executives on terminated employees which indicated that productivity studies were irrelevant because they were done on older workers who remained employed and were, therefore, available for survey and likely to have been so selected as to offer equivalent productivity.

Heavy unemployment of the older worker as a group in Massachusetts also testifies to the likelihood that those not employed were less productive than younger workers.

Thus, the "the Older Worker staff after evidencing the job developing difficulties facing the "hard core" older worker and the retired older worker or the older worker who is close to retirement age, undertaken in June of 1967 a more personalized job development methodology for all applicants.

The case study of Mr. B. represents the successful method of job development and placement utilized by the Older Worker staff from June of 1967 through July 31, 1968.

CASE OF MR. B

Mr. B, a sixty-one year old male, was referred to the Older Worker Program at the John F. Kennedy Family Service Center, Inc., by a local rehabilitation agency. Aside from chronic alcoholism, Mr. B has no other disabilities and is assessed as being in extremely good physical condition.

HISTORY OF EMPLOYMENT AND ALCOHOLISM

The Older Worker Program Director discussed in detail Mr. B's alcoholic problem and its influence on his unstable work habits and poor job performance. The multiple services of the John F. Kennedy Family Service Center, Inc., and the special procedures utilized to help him find employment were explained.

Mr. B worked as a clerk accountant in a prominent Boston bank for 17 years before he joined the U.S. Army in 1942. Upon his discharge in October, 1945, Mr. B lived on his savings and drank heavily. Lacking funds in April, 1946, he sought employment and was hired as a porter for a large Boston firm where he remained for seven years. Since 1953, he has worked as a houseman in a Boston hotel for two years, and has held other similar jobs for shorter periods of time.

Mr. B's drinking first became a problem in 1940 and grew more severe after his discharge from the Army in 1945. His heavy drinking resulted in job losses and an inability to function in or maintain any job. His single status and loneliness was and has been a factor in his drinking behavior.

Mr. B was referred by the Older Worker Program Director to the Kennedy Center's Social Service Department for pre-placement evaluation which revealed that Mr. B had ego strength and was well motivated for employment. Employment was recommended under minimum pressure conditions.

JOB INTERVIEWING AND TESTING

Mr. B was most cooperative and confident of his ability to learn whatever job was offered to him. Various occupational tests and the Kuder Vocational and Kuder Personal were administered. (The Wonderlic was not given because General Aptitude Test Battery (GATB) Scores were available. He received a G-score of 98, indicating average intelligence.)

The Kuder Vocational revealed a preference for working with machines and tools and activities requiring precision and accuracy rather than activities involving abstract reasoning and computational skills. The Kuder Personal verified preference for working with things rather than ideas. He preferred working alone rather than with a large group and was not interested in a supervisory role. Mr. B expressed a desire to work with machines, but realized that he had neither skills nor experience in this field.

JOB SCREENING

Intensive job screening was begun. A personal interview with a prospective employer was arranged to explain the Older Worker Program and discuss specific duties, hours and salary of the position available.

A description of the applicant and his problem, his steps toward self rehabilitation, and his qualifications for employment were discussed with the employer. A tour of the work area followed for a first-hand evaluation of work environment.

COUNSELING AND PLACEMENT

The employment counselor contacted the counselor at the rehabilitation agency to discuss the available opening before it was presented to Mr. B. Mr. B expressed special interest in the position available at a drug company and an interview with the personnel manager informed of Mr. B's case was arranged.

Transportation to the interview was provided by a member of the Older Worker Program staff after confirming the appointment with the personnel manager who upon arrival was unable to see Mr. B. Another interviewer, unfamiliar with the case, questioned Mr. B about his past employment and asked him to fill out an application instead of discussing the available opening. Mr. B became very nervous since he was unable to recall the dates and locations of his recent work experiences.

Mr. B's disappointment with the interview, the 20 minute wait and his growing state of anxiety seemed unnecessarily provoking. The application was left at the main desk.

The return to the city gave the counselor an opportunity to help Mr. B cope with the confusion and disappointment brought on by the interview and to present several alternatives to him with the search for other openings to be started the following morning. Mr. B was left near several department stores to shop during his two hour wait for the bus.

Mr. B's rehabilitation counselor called the following morning with news that Mr. B had returned on the bus and had not been drinking. He believed that this indicated Mr. B's ability to handle a stressful situation and confirmed his readiness for employment. He felt the concern and support of the Older Worker Program staff was a contributing factor to Mr. B's success.

Additional companies were visited and jobs were screened. An interview was arranged with an interested manager of a small button company who had been informed of Mr. B's case. Mr. B, accompanied by a member of the Older Worker staff, was interviewed by the manager. The foreman gave him a tour of the department demonstrating the duties he was to perform. Mr. B was most enthusiastic about the job and was hired as an assistant machinist.

FOLLOW-UP

A two-week follow-up indicated that Mr. B enjoyed working with machines and learning new skills. He liked his fellow employees. Mr. B's employer was pleased with work and said that he was quick to learn his new skill. Mr. B's counselor had visited him on the job and thought the work was therapeutic and very interesting to Mr. B. Attempts are being made to enter Mr. B in a halfway house which will facilitate transportation and assimilate community living. A continuous follow-up will be made every two weeks.

PLACEMENT

Counseling and Placement Procedure

Every applicant to the Older Worker Program is first registered with the John F. Kennedy Family Service Center, Inc., utilizing the J.F.K. Registration Form.

The new applicant is given a Skill Inventory Form and a Health Questionnaire to complete prior to the initial interview.

The applicant is interviewed by professional counselors. At an initial interview, the counselor evaluates the personal and family problems that may affect employability and, if appropriate, a referral is made on a Referral Form.

Three references (past employer or personal) are requested from the applicant which are immediately processed. Evaluation of past work record is discussed with the applicant.

The applicant's physical ability is assessed by a review and discussion of the health questionnaire and personal observation by the counselor. Medical and psychological evaluations are requested by the counselor if physical disabilities will impair employability utilizing the release of medical information..

The Kuder Preference Record-Vocational and the Kuder Preference-Personal (both interest inventories) and Wonderlic Personnel Test (a problem solving abilities test) are offered to all applicants.

Evaluation of test results, job interests and openings for which the applicant may qualify are discussed with the applicant by the professional counselor.

Applicants who are in the referral status are not considered for job placement until a medical or Social Services evaluation and/or communication from outside agencies indicates that the applicant is employable.

The professional counselor and vocational counselor review the results of the initial interview (e.g., attitude, motivation, skill, work experience, references, test scores, and personal or family problems that may affect employability) and make suggestions regarding potential areas in which the applicant shows interest and ability.

The professional counselor introduces the applicant to the vocational counselor, and assists the applicant in completion of the Older Worker Registration Form and Employment History Form. The vocational counselor evaluates the applicant's employability on Counselor Evaluation Form with the professional counselor and selects various suitable job openings.

Employers are then contacted by the vocational counselor to ascertain:

— if the position is still open; and,

— job specifications and description of duties — Employer Inquiry form; if the position is still available, the vocational counselor then reviews the specific job requirements with the applicant.

If the applicant advises that he can perform and desires the job, the vocational counselor and professional counselor may personally visit the employer on the applicant's behalf.

A follow-up on the date of interview to determine whether placement was accomplished is done by the vocational counselor using the Telephone Follow-Up Form. Follow-up on all direct placements is accomplished on a one, three and six month basis by the vocational counselor — Employer Questionnaire.

The case study of Mr. B (Section of Job Development) illustrates the counseling and placement techniques and procedures utilized by the Older Worker staff for all regular and "hard core" applicants.

Discussion

As of July 31, 1968, a total of 667 placements had been made by the John F. Kennedy Older Worker Program. Three hundred and seven (307) were direct placements, i.e., Kennedy Center placed, and 360 were developed as indirect placements, i.e., the applicants found the job themselves. The indirect placements are, in large measure, due to the enrollees' association with the Older Worker Program which provided sufficient motivation, confidence, and "know how" enabled the applicants' search for jobs. This increased level of confidence is substantiated by the fact that almost 80 percent of the indirect placements were developed through the efforts of the applicants rather than through the efforts of a formal organization such as another agency or union. Table VIII indicates the methods used by the indirect placement in his job search.

The skill levels of the direct and indirect placements are shown in Table IX. Over 68 percent of these placements either maintained or upgraded the skills that the applicant had in his previous occupation. In addition, over 40 percent of those who had last been in unskilled positions were upgraded. This is all the more remarkable in view of the advanced age and spotty employment of the bulk of the applicants. The exact placements of the applicants, relative to their last skill level, are indicated in Figure 1, Last Skill Level Compared to Placement Skill Level.

Those placed exhibit roughly the same characteristics as the entire population; however, the incidence of "hard core" characteristics is, on the average, somewhat lower among the

TABLE VIII

INDIRECT PLACEMENTS

Methods Used to Develop Jobs*

	Number	Percent
Personal Application	40	37.4
Friend, Neighbor, Politician, Relative	31	28.9
Newspaper	24	22.4
D.E.S.	5	4.7
Business Associations, Former Employer, Other Agency	5	4.7
Union	2	1.9

*Based on a sample of 107 from a population of 360.

TABLE IX

SKILL LEVELS OF DIRECT AND INDIRECT PLACEMENTS

	Direct Placements	Indirect Placements
Professional	4	34
Middle Management	9	32
Clerical and Sales	15	53
Skilled	7	15
Semi-Skilled	14	15
Menial Clerical	60	46
Service, Protection, Health	19	21
Service, Food Processing	15	9
Service, Building	78	36
Unskilled	86	90
Blank	0	9
TOTAL	307	360

FIGURE 1

TYPE OF PLACEMENT		UPGRADE	DOWNGRADE	SAME
	D		6.2	12.5
Professional and Managerial				
	I		21.9	59.4
	D		17.0	2.0
Middle Management				
	I	10.6	36.3	34.0
	D	6.0	10.0	14.0
Clerical and Sales				
	I	8.0	16.0	46.0
	D		9.1	27.3
Skilled				
	I	4.5	22.7	36.4
	D	2.9	38.2	20.6
Semi-Skilled				
	I	5.9	14.7	17.7
	D	1.4	10.0	30.0
Menial Clerical				
	I	5.7	18.6	34.3
	D	11.1	27.8	11.1
Service, Protective, Health				
	I	5.6	11.1	33.3
	D	11.1	27.8	11.1
Service, Food Processing				
	I	11.1	16.7	22.2
	D	12.3	10.5	29.8
Service, Building				
	I	12.3	12.3	22.8
	D	27.6		21.9
Unskilled				
	I	10.5		40.0

D=Direct   I=Indirect

applicants who were placed. There is a significant difference between the charcteristics of the direct and indirect placements. As shown in Table X, the direct placements were on the average older, more disadvantaged, less educated, and had a higher incidence of "hard core" characteristics than the indirect placements. In addition, there was a higher incidence of females and of residents of the target group in the direct placement populations. In view of these statistics, it is not surprising that there are significant differences in the skill levels of the two groups with the "average" indirect placement possessing significantly higher skills than the "average" direct placement.

TABLE X

*Selected Characteristics of the Population
(N=640), the Direct Placements (N=173) and
the Indirect Placements (N=215)*

	Population	Direct Placements	Indirect Placements
SEX			
Percent Males	69.4	61.9	73.0
Percent Females	30.6	38.1	73.0
RESIDENCE			
Percent Target	31.1	42.2	23.3
Percent Comparison	68.9	57.8	76.7
Average Age (in years)	60.0	60.3	58.2
Mean Education (in years)	11.2	10.5	11.8
Mean Monthly Income	$75	$70	$80
Percentage with "Hard Core" Characteristics	48%	49.7%	34.0%

As shown in Table XI the direct placements had, in general, lower primary skill levels than the population as a whole while the indirect placements had generally *higher* skill levels.

The status of the enrollees in the program as of July 31, 1968, is shown in Table XII.

In the period from July, 1966, to June, 1967, the Kennedy Center developed jobs, in part, through a form letter. During this period, 255 companies were contacted and 2,055 positions were developed. (See Table XIII). The distribution of jobs developed was not congruent with the distribution of the primary skills of the applicants; for example, while 116 applicants had primary skills in the professional, managerial, and middle management levels, only 20 positions were developed in these skills. After June, 1967, the Older Worker Program undertook a more personalized job development methodology in which the skills and desires of the applicant were closely matched to the type of job developed

TABLE XI

PERCENT DISTRIBUTION OF SKILL LEVELS

	Total Population N=640	Direct Placements N=173	Indirect Placements N=215
Professional, Managerial	8.9	4.1	12.3
Middle Management	9.4	1.7	15.3
Clerical and Sales	10.8	8.1	15.7
Skilled	5.6	5.2	7.0
Semi-Skilled	9.5	12.1	7.0
Menial Clerical	16.2	21.4	12.0
Service, Protective & Health	3.6	5.8	3.7
Service, Food Processing	4.5	5.2	2.8
Service, Building	9.5	15.6	5.1
Unskilled	22.0	20.8	19.1

TABLE XII

STATUS OF THE ENROLLEES AS OF JULY 31, 1968

	NUMBER	PERCENT
Direct Placement	84	13.12
Indirect Placement	183	28.59
Active Placement	25	3.90
Inactive	21	3.28
Retired	28	4.37
Not Interested	48	7.50
No Response	80	12.50
Other	171	26.74
TOTAL	640	100%

for him. Over 60 percent of the placements either upgraded or maintained the applicants previous skill levels, attest to the success of this new approach.

TABLE XIII
Results of Job Development Mailer
from July, 1966, to June, 1967
Number of Positions Developed by Skill Level

Professional and Managerial	1
Middle Management	19
Clerical and Sales	169
Skilled	225
Semi-Skilled	376
Menial Clerical	242
Unskilled	513
Service, Protective	103
Service, Building	92
Service, Food Processing	315
TOTAL	2,055

Massachusetts Division of Employment Security

In the period July 1, 1966, through July 31, 1968, Division of Employment Security referred 151 applicants to the Older Worker Program. Four hundred and eighty-nine (489) applicants were referred from other sources classified here as non-Division of Employment Security.

Only 3.3 percent or five applicants referred by Division of Employment Security were from the target group.

Sixty-eight and eight tenths percent (68.8%) or 98 of the Division of Employment Security referrals were between the ages of 61 and 65 as compared to 39.6 percent or 194 non-Division of Employment Security applicants.

Over 90 percent of Division of Employment Security applicants and 87.4 percent of non-Division of Employment Security applicants claimed to be in excellent or good health. However, 43 percent of the Division of Employment Security applicants and 51.1 percent of the non-Division of Employment Security applicants were classified as "hard core." Division of Employment Security "hard core" applicants had a higher percent of physical disabilities (heart trouble, arthritis, etc.) 36 or 24 percent as compared to non-Division of Employment Security applicants 83 or 16.9 percent. Seven or 4.7 percent of the Division of Employment Security applicants were alcoholic as compared to 91 or 18.6 percent for the non-Division of Employment Security applicants. Eleven (11) or 7.3 percent Division of Employment Security applicants were found to be unmotivated or presented unrealistic restrictions (wanted special hours, would not travel any distance and demanded top wages).

Nine (9) or six percent stated that they were only registering because they were told that in order to collect unemployment benefits they must register for the Kennedy Center Older Worker Program. The non-Division of Employment Security applicants presenting the same "hard core" characteristics totaled 21 or only 4.3 percent of the "hard core" applicants.

The primary skill level of the Division of Employment Security applicants in the professional managerial and middle management levels was three times as great as the non-Division of Employment Security applicants or 56 or 37.1 percent Division of Employment Security compared to 61 or 12.4 percent non-Division of Employment Security.

In the clerical and sales, skilled and semi-skilled for Division of Employment Security referred 51 or 33.8 percent. In skill levels such as menial clerical, service protective, service food, and service building 23 or 15.2 percent were Division of Employment Security applicants and 193 or 39.5 percent were non-Division of Employment Security applicants.

Division of Employment Security referred 21 or only 13.9 percent applicants who were classified as unskilled as compared to 120 or 24.5 percent non-Division of Employment Security.

There were 52 or 34.4 percent Division of Employment Security applicants who reported no income, as compared to 168 or 38.0 percent of the non-Division of Employment Security applicants. Social Security Pension, disability pensions and Old Age Assistance were claimed as a source of income for 75 or 50.3 percent of the Division of Employment Security applicants, while only 156 or 31.9 percent of the non-Division of Employment Security applicants claimed these same sources of income. The large number of Division of Employment Security applicants receiving pension and Social Security income reflects the need for a supplemental income for people 60 years of age and over. It also includes the problem Division of Employment Security is having finding part-time positions for the aging group.

Division of Employment Security referrals are characterized by *one* applicant being in an older age group, (68.8 percent were 61

years of age and over) and over *two* requesting part-time incomes
to supplement pension and Social Security benefits. Seventy-five
(75) or 50.3 percent were on some type of retirement benefits; three
were in poor physical condition (raising the question as to how
these people are able to function in industry even on a part-time
basis) and 36 or 24 percent had one or more physical disabilities.

The distribution of characteristics for those enrollees recruited
by Division of Employment Security differs from those recruited
by other means. The 151 Division of Employment Security
enrollees were, on the average, older, better educated, possessed
fewer "hard core" characteristics, had much higher primary skill
levels, and relatively higher income than the non-Division of
Employment Security recruits (See Table XIV).

TABLE XIV

	DES	NON-DES
Average Age	62.36	58.52
Average Grade Completed	12.48	10.80
Average Income (per month)	$85.00	$70.00
Primary Skill Level		
Percent in Professional, Managerial, Clerical and Skilled Occupations	58.30%	27.30%
Percent Unskilled	13.90%	24.50%
Percent "Hard Core"	43.00%	50.10%

Part-Time Employment

The economic loss of highly experienced and skilled older
workers seeking part-time employment is staggering. This year
24,000,000 older Americans will be eligible for Social Security
benefits. Many of these individuals are in good mental and
physical health and are either in need of work due to economic
necessity or desire to continue employment.

The part-time employment needs of the older workers cannot
be entirely met by industry. Pension plans, a youth-oriented
society, industrial inability to redesign jobs and Social Security

laws which reduce benefits when an older worker's earned income reaches $1,680 contribute to the dilemma facing the older worker desirous of part-time employment. The need for job opportunities and healthy retired workers has been proclaimed by President Johnson:

> "Perhaps the greatest need of age is the need to know that one's contributions are still valued. In a society where youth is so highly prized, older men and women need to know that their wisdom and experience are also important to their fellow citizens. Their contributions are one of our nation's most valuable assets — a resource that should be celebrated by every generation of Americans."

In recognition of this severe problem, the Department of Labor is creating 3,000 job opportunities for older workers (unemployed citizens over 55) in 1969. This is only the first step in assisting these life long tax payers from the status of second class citizens. Federal, state, local government and private agencies must recognize, develop, and implement programs which will assist the aging older worker.

The Older Worker Program's experience with the part-time applicant substantiates this economic loss. The need for part-time employment for older workers, especially those persons over 62 years of age and in need of funds to supplement inadequate pensions and Social Security benefits, for additional income for full support or supplemental purposes was revealed by 198 or 30.93 percent of the total registered applicants.

Between July 1, 1966, and August 31, 1968, 132 or 20.63 percent of the registered applicants requested part-time employment, another 66 or 10.31 percent also stated a preference for part-time work. However, they would accept an immediate full-time position with a higher wage, thus jeopardizing their pension and Social Security benefits.

Because of the scarcity of part-time positions in the Greater Boston area, especially at the higher skill levels, the staff devised two experimental plans which hopefully would develop part-time jobs for the older worker.

The first plan involved following up our contacts with employers, particularly hospitals, institutions, hotels, manufacturers, and other service occupations recommending an experimental plan whereby they would hire two workers for one job to work alternate weeks. The second plan was implemented whereby an employee would work until he had reached his maximum benefit at which time, a second employee was made available.

Both plans were presented and accepted by both large and small service, insurance, and small manufacturing companies who were willing to arrange part-time work for the applicant meeting their qualifications.

The Older Worker Program successfully implemented both programs in the placement of the unskilled older workers. However, those Older Worker applicants who had higher skill levels could not utilize either plan because it was impossible to find a second applicant to work alternate weeks and/or the first placed applicant had not reached maximum benefits. Part-time placements either directly or indirectly were secured by 61 or 30.81 percent of the applicants requesting part-time work. Part-time job development by the Older Worker staff was difficult to accomplish because:

1. Part-time positions available to older workers were generally in the lower skilled jobs (service-protective and health, service-food and food processing, and unskilled) and in most cases, were turned down by the majority of enrollees who had higher primary skill levels and could not accept a position that would downgrade their skill level.
2. Many applicants stating the need for part-time jobs or supplemental income turned down job opportunities when faced with the reality of possible loss of Social Security benefits by going over the earned income allowed by Social Security ($1,680 maximum earned income allowed to Social Security recipients).
3. Other older worker applicants refused part-time positions when faced with the actual dollar income gain from working part-time.

Future experimentation with job development and placement of older workers seeking part-time employment by state or federal experimental or services programs will only contradict their original intent, i.e., supplemental income for those on pension or

Social Security, as long as the present Social Security Law imposes limits on earned income.

"Under the present law a qualified recipient can receive an *unlimited* amount of income from investments, interest, rents, royalties or other so-called unearned income, without any loss of his Social Security benefits; whereas any earned income (that is income earned by working) exceeding $1680 penalizes his Social Security benefits eventually eliminating them entirely. This penalty is in force until a worker attains the age of 72, when the law provides he can now go to work and earn all he is able to and he can keep his Social Security benefits.

This distinction of type of income severely penalizes the person who cannot live on his Social Security benefits in addition to the $1,680 he may earn; therefore, he must forfeit his "benefits" (which he paid for in compulsory taxes and which were matched by his employer for his benefit as a form of fringe benefit) and continue to work to support himself until he is 72 years old, all the while continuing to pay Social Security taxes (1)."

Manpower Development and Training Act Training

In March of 1962, a Manpower Development and Training Act Job Training Program was designed to provide workers with new skills, to upgrade present skills, to meet the job needs of workers displaced by automation, industrial relocation, and shifts in market demands.

Training was received through vocational courses in local trade, business, and service schools in the Greater Boston area and throughout the state, commensurate with the occupational needs in the area or state, on-the-job training requirements or both. A training allowance was provided for the trainees.

The Older Worker Program, in cooperation with the Massachusetts Division of Employment Security, utilized the Manpower Development Training Act Program. During the period from July 1, 1966, to July 31, 1968, only twelve (12) Older

---

1. Philip Saponaro, *Democratic Town Committee*, Natwick, Massachusetts.

Worker applicants were accepted for the Manpower Development and Training Act Program.

However, 265 or 41.41 percent of the Older Worker applicants interviewed indicated they would accept training courses suited to their particular interest and aptitudes.

The Older Worker placement counselors felt that in 50 percent of the applicants indicating a desire for training could have had their employability enhanced by taking an appropriate course.

The failure to introduce the Older Worker applicants to Manpower Development and Training Act can be attributed to the following facts:

— In the first stages of the Older Worker Program, the staff made few attempts to develop any interest in Manpower Development and Training Act training program; and,

— Early Older Worker Program procedures had provided no measure of the actual interest on the part of the older worker in training programs.

It should also be pointyed out that Manpower Development and Training Act experiences highlighted the following additional limitations:

1. The limited number of work stations limited the enrollment. Only a small percentage of the unemployed could be accommodated in the various vocational courses.

2. Many of the training schools were equipped to train high school youth and operated on sex or seven hours a day for only nine months of the year. These facilities were not available for adult training except during the evening or night hours. Experienced day school teachers were not available for these evening classes, which further reduced the quality of the training program.

3. The vocational schools did not offer comprehensive training programs. Some, for example, concentrated on the metal working trade; some on the wood working crafts; and still others on the service occupations. Consequently many of these schools could not meet the demands for comprehensive training programs due to a lack of diversified training programs. (Approximately 25-30 percent of the training courses offered from July 1, 1966, to July 31, 1968 were adaptable to the future employment development of the

older worker.)

4. A further consideration was the time lag between date of application and the commencement of a training program. The type of system predicated on "saving up" people for training until a sizeable class is assembled is considered wasteful and seemed to disregard the pressing needs of the unemployed individual.

Results of Manpower Development and Training Act Training

Of the 12 applicants who accepted Manpower Development and Training Act Training, three took training courses below their last occupations skill level. Only seven applicants completed the training courses, four staying at the skill level offered by taking the course, one applicant being upgraded and two accepting employment below their skill level.

Employment after taking the Manpower Development and Training Act course was secured by six of the applicants through their own efforts, one applicant returned to the Center and was directly placed. The status of the 12 Older Worker applicants sent by the Kennedy Center for Manpower Development and Training Act traineeship as of July 31, 1968, is indicated in Table XV.

TABLE XV

MDTA COMPLETED COURSE

Status of Trainees as of July 31, 1968

Direct Placement	1
Indirect Placement	4
Still In Course	1
Active	1
Not Interested	1
Deceased	1
Physically Unable	2
Blank-no information	1
TOTAL	12

TERMINATIONS

Of the 667 placements made since the beginning of the John F.

Kennedy Family Service Center's Older Worker Program, 253 were still employed as of July 31, 1968. The effective overall job retention rate was approximately 40 percent. However, the job retention rate of the indirect placements was significantly higher than that of the direct placements. Only 84 out of the 307 direct placements were still employed, while 169 out of the 360 indirect placements were employed as of the end of the contract. This bears out the fact that the indirect placements as a group were more motivated, confident, and suited for a working environment than the direct placement group.

Out of the total of 408 terminations, 147 or 36 percent were terminated by the employer while 261 or 64 percent resigned. Of those who were termianted by the employer over 30 percent had "hard core" characteristics — maily alcoholism. Of those who resigned, less than 5 percent possessed "hard core" characteristics. Those applicants with "hard core" characteristics were not only the most difficult to place but also experienced the greatest difficulty in retaining a job.

Termination rate by age, shows that the highest termination rates occur in the age groups 51-55, and in the age groups over 66 years of age. Similarly, the highest rate of termination by an employer is experienced by those in the 45-55 age bracket and those 66 and over. A partial explanation of this fact is that the highest incidence of alcoholism occurs in the 51-55 age bracket.

It is interesting to note that 35 percent of the terminations and resignations among the direct placements were caused by "hard core" symptoms while only 21 percent of the terminations and resignations occurred among the indirect placements. This confirms the initial hypothesis that the direct placement suffers from a significantly higher incidence of "hard core" problems.

THE MULTI-SERVICE FRAMEWORK

The Older Worker Program's evolution as an integral component of the Kennedy Center's multi-service framework has made available comprehensive, coordinated and continuous services for each Older Worker applicant and his family.

The Older Worker staff, equipped with the coordinated and

diversified expertise of the total Kennedy Center staff, has been able:

— to identify, counsel and seek job placement for the individual 45 and over;

— to recommend any one of the multi-services in the resolution of short and long term problems which intervene in or prohibit the effective placement for and maintenance of employment; and,

— to maintain, restore, and support the individual applicant in the process of service and solution to his multiple problems.

In particular, the employment counseling process afforded the counselor an opportunity to learn the applicant's expected and realistic employment goals; to judge the applicant's employability in terms of past work history, skill, work habits and attitudes; and to determine the concomitant socio-economic, familial and individual idiosyncrasies affecting his employment. Should any one or a combination of these factors restrict or prohibit effective employment counseling and placement, the counselor referred the applicant to the appropriate multi-service component for attention.

The employment counselor's understanding of the applicant's life style and the relevant forces of his human environment enhanced, his ability to perceive the total individual in his search for employment and his use of multi-service referral to facilitate the employment search and resolution.

Table XVI indicates the Kennedy Center's multi-services to which the "hard core" and "non hard core" enrollees were referred within the Center.

Ninety or 29.03 percent of the "hard core" enrollees were inter-agency referrals, i.e., hospitals, alcoholic clinics and other agencies. In most cases, employment evaluation was accomplished by Kennedy Center Older Worker counselors in conjunction with the caseworker of the referral agency or by consultation with members of the Kennedy Center Social Service staff.

There were 97 or 31.3 percent of the "hard core" who were not involved in either inter- or intra-agency referral. This was due to the fact that those registered in the Older Worker Program during

TABLE XVI

KENNEDY CENTER INTRA-AGENCY REFERRALS

	Non Hard Core (N=330)	Hard Core (N=310)
Incidence of Referrals	6	137
Social Service	1	107
Legal Aid	3	20
Surplus Food	2	6
Elderly Services	0	4
No Referral	0	97

the early part of the program were not classified as "hard core" until follow-up revealed some type of disability. Those applicants were requersted to return to the Center and to avail themselves of the Kennedy Center's multi-service referrals. Few applicants responded to this request indicating the need for strong "outreach" techniques in future programs.

TALENTS

At the inception of the Older Worker Program, the Older Worker staff acutely aware of the difficulty the unemployed and underemployed managerial and professional older worker have in seeking re-entry into the world of work, established a self-help organization to assist these applicants with successful re-entry into the labor market, called Talents.

A group setting provided a source of interaction for the members and became a vital supportive measure for their morale. The meetings focused upon the common barriers shared by the Talents members and provided insight concerning the directions to be taken in obtaining gainful employment and upgrading. Talents met once a week under the guidance and direction of an Older Worker staff person assigned exclusively to the professional

and managerial applicants. This staff member's function was to:
— find employment for the unemployed professional and managerial applicants;
— upgrade professional and managerial applicant who believe that their present employment is not commensurate with their abilities and skills; and,
— introduce new professional and managerial applicants to Talents.

This staff member was made available to all professional and managerial applicants two hours prior to each meeting. This permitted the Talents member and new applicants to discuss recent job openings and to prepare and send resumes to prospective employers.

The regular counseling and placement techniques for professional and managerial applicants, resume services, newspaper clipping service, and company visits on behalf of individual applicants, have been successful in returning these applicants to employment. However, these regular counseling techniques did not prove adequate in dealing with all professional and managerial applicants.

"Hard core" professional and managerial applicants have benefited from the same procedure used for all "hard core" applicants, i.e., intensified counseling, referral to Social Services, Legal Aid and psychological and medical evaluations.

Several activities and techniques were devised to assuage the anxieties and frustrations attending the employment problems encountered by the Talents member. These activities included:
— morale building;
— counseling to develop new areas for employment;
— exploration of possible business ventures;
— group participation in seeking employment openings for other members; and,
— development of group interests through outside contacts.

Particular techniques included:
— *Thumbnail Sketch:* This sketch was a brief description of each members's employment background given to various employers by Talents representatives as they conducted their own employment search;

— *Resume:* Resumes were made for each Talents member. These resumes were first criticized and improved upon by other group members before they were sent to an employer; and,

— *Mailing Service:* Talents members clipped those help wanted ads from Boston newspapers which met their job specifications. These clippings were then sent to an Older Worker employment counselor who answered these ads by sending the prospective employer a covering letter.

During the period from July 1, 1966, to December 31, 1967, meeting were held at the John F. Kennedy Family Service Center, Inc., every Thursday evening. The members elected officers to preside at each meeting and drafted by-laws. The original purpose of job placement and upgrading was disregarded by a majority of Talents members who believed that industry would not hire them in positions for which they felt qualified. There were 10 to 15 professional managerial older workers who continually attended meetings, and only one was unemployed. All believed they were underemployed.

The Older Worker Program's experience with this group indicated that each member was employed in a position commensurate with his professional abilities and physical well-being.

The exploration of a joint business venture dominated eight months deliberation on the part of Talents members. Various business opportunities were discussed. However, the establishment of a small business never developed because of their inability to obtain agreement on the type of business, disagreement concerning the method of organization, lack of adequate leadership to assume the responsibility of final decision, and reluctance to invest capital necessary.

There were 118 registered Older Worker applicant who stated their last occupation was professional management or middle management skill level, from July 1, 1966, to July 31, 1968. All of these applicants were informed of the Talents program; however, only 48 attended more than one meeting and only 10 to 15 attended on a regular basis. The counselor's attempts to recruit new members were unsuccessful because:

— the objectives of the Talents group did not comply with the new professional and managerial applicant's goal which was job placement;

— unemployed or underemployed professional and managerial applicants have all expressed a desire for immediate employment; and,

— once a professional and managerial applicant accepted a position, he generally showed no further interest in Talents.

Continued efforts were conducted to uncover the barriers of unemployed and underemployed professional and managerial older workers in finding satisfactory re-entry or upgrading into the labor market.

The Older Worker staff contacted by mail 255 companies in an attempt to develop jobs for the professional managerial Older Worker applicant registered in the program. The total number of jobs developed in the first ten months of the program totaled 2,355 and only one top management position was offered by a community action program. There were only 19 middle management positions and all of these were located in small businesses (employing less than 50 people) or in institutions or hospitals.

The Older Worker staff consulted with personnel executives in both manufacturing, insurance and retail industries to determine industry's reluctance in offering professional management and middle management positions to older workers.

The personnel executives were asked to discuss the problems they encountered in hiring the professional managerial candidate. Their reluctance stems from one or more of the following reasons:

— Many found that the general health of the older worker tends to be poor. They are overweight and have a generally neglected appearance.

— The professional and managerial applicant, in many instances, claims years of experience. When questioned or tested, there was found to be a definite lack of knowledge of up-to-date technology.

— Many found the older worker professional managerial applicant unwilling to accept company training programs that were offered. When a training program was acceptable to this applicant, he did poorly in comparison with younger trainees. The older worker felt that he had more experience and subsequently his attitude toward training was poor.

— Many company executives stated that they preferred to train and promote younger men from within the company in order to keep morale and incentive high.

Contrary to past experience, insurance and pension plan costs were not the primary concern of the company executives interviewed. One insurance company executive stated that the question of increased fringe benefit cost in hiring older workers is often overlooked and widely misunderstood. He stated that insurance and annuity cost increase with age; however, it is not necessarily true that the costs involved for older persons will be several times higher. Age is one variable; however, other factors such as years of service and average salary are likewise very important.

Another important variable is the "number of years of service" for which pension costs are being incurred. This insurance executive gave the following explanation as an example:

> One employee hired at age 25 and retiring at age 65 receives a pension based on 40 years of service. Four employees hired at age 55 who retire at age 65 also represent pension obligations based on 40 years of service. Now consider in comparing costs that this employee hired at age 25 will usually have reached a substantially higher salary level and his pension and its associated costs will reflect this. The employee hired at age 55 will usually have entered at a much lower average salary and the total cost to the employer will not necessarily be several times higher.

Most professional and managerial applicants (45-60) who were unemployed through merger or other reasons, found employment sooner if they had education and experience commensurate with the position, good health, mental and physical, appropriate appearance, willingness to accept new ideas, and willingness to accept company training programs.

The experience of Talents has suggested that under direct supervision, these professional and managerial people benefited not only from available multi-services within the Kennedy Center, but also from the group setting which provided a supportive atmosphere for the investigation of new job opportunities.

APPENDIX I

BENEFIT COST ANALYSIS

FORMULA A

The benefit-cost ratio can then be calculated via the following formula:

$$\frac{B}{C} = \sum_{S} [I_a - I_b][A_m][N_s]$$

COSTS OF THE PROGRAM

WHERE:

B = Benefits
C = Costs
I_a = Average monthly income after placement
I_b = Average monthly income before placement
A_m = Average tenure in job
N_s = Number of applicants in each stratum
S = Direct placements, indirect placements, case closed

Fitting the data in Table I into this formula leads to the following results:

$$\frac{B}{C} = \frac{[\$358 - \$108][11.4 \text{ months}][84] + [393 - 84][15.2][183] + [212 - 68]}{[5][327]} = 3.44$$

$$\$250,000$$

FORMULA B

$$\frac{B}{C} = \text{Present Value of } \sum_S \left[I_a - I_b\right]\left[A_m\right]\left[N_s\right][.10]$$

COST OF THE PROGRAM

WHERE:

I_a = Average monthly income after placement

I_{bf} = Average monthly income before placement

sA_m = Five years in the job

N_s = Number of applicants in each stratum

Present value factor = 6%

Inserting the data into the formula leads to the following results:

$$\frac{B}{C} = \text{Present Value} \left[\left[358 - 108\right]\left[60 \text{ months}\right]\left[84\right][.10]\right] + \text{Present Value}$$

$$\left[393 - 84\right]\left[60 \text{ months}\right]\left[83\right][.10] + \text{Present Value} \left[\left[212 - 67\right]\left[60\right]\left[372\right][10]\right] =$$

$$\frac{417,752 + 1,337,137}{\$250,000} = 4.38$$

APPENDIX II

STANDARD OPERATING PROCEDURE

Older Worker Training and Employment Program
John F. Kennedy Family Service Center, Inc.

 I. *REQUIREMENTS FOR QUALIFICATIONS FOR OLDER WORKER PROGRAM*
    Applicant must be forty-five (45) years of age or over.
 II. *REGISTRATION OF OLDER WORKER APPLICANTS*
    Applicants must first register with the receptionist at the John F. Kennedy Family Service Center, Inc.
 III. *INTAKE PROCEDURE*
    A. New applicants are introduced to the Older Worker

staff member who will:

1. take the applicant to a private room for an intake interview;
2. complete the forms on behalf of the applicant if the applicant cannot write or is physically disabled;
3. request that the applicant return the next day if the applicant is intoxicated at the time of interview;
4. acquaint the applicant with all the services available at the Kennedy Center; Legal Aid, Surplus Food, Youth Services, Family Counseling, Elderly Services and Testing;
5. discuss the general health of the applicant as it relates to employment; (if a more complete medical history on the applicant's physical condition would be more helpful, the interviewer may request the applicant to complete the Health Questionnaire or require a medical evaluation from the applicant's physician. Applicants requiring a medical evaluation will not be registered until an affirmative evaluation stating that the applicant is employable is received.)
6. request the applicant to submit the names of two of his most recent employers for a reference check. If same cannot be supplied, two personal references will be requested. The interviewer will arrange to have the reference check done by another staff member while the applicant is in the intake process. If there are any contradictions uncovered by the reference check, these will be discussed openly with the applicant without revealing the source of information;
7. discuss with the applicant personal problems that may affect his employability and in the event that an inter- or intra-agency referral is appropriate, this will be made by the initial interviewer before any action regarding employment is taken; and,
8. discuss general areas of employment and introduce the applicant to a vocational counselor after briefing

the latter on the specifics of the case.

IV. *EMPLOYMENT INTERVIEW*

  A. The vocational counselor will:

    1. ask the applicant to complete the first section of the Application Form and the counselor will complete the remaining sections of the form along with:

      a. Employment History Form

      b. Evaluation Form;

    2. all forms are given to the secretary and an Older Worker Program registration number is assigned and recorded; and,

    3. conduct a more in-depth interview regarding employment, and will review with the job development specialist the specific work history, interests, and abilities to determine the best placement for the applicant, and discuss various positions available which may interest the applicant.

V. *PLACEMENT PROCEDURE*

  A. The job development specialist and/or the vocational counselor will personally develop and screen possible openings corresponding to the qualifications and requirements of the applicant either by telephone or by personal visit to the prospective employer.

  B. The vocational counselor will then discuss the job with the applicant, carefully explaining all the details, i.e., benefits and job requirements. If the applicant is *interested,* a definite interview with the employer will be arranged.

  C. At this time, the employer should be made aware of the applicant's qualifications and in the case of a "hard core" applicant, the employer should also be made aware of the applicant's problems.

  D. Prior to the interview, the vocational counselor may write a letter of introduction to the employer and furnish the applicant with a copy of same, or in case of "hard core" applicants, may accompany them to the interview.

E. The counselor will follow up on the results of the interview, and if the applicant has been hired will contact the employer on the date specified to ascertain that the applicant is now employed.

F. The proper dictation will be given to the secretary.

VI. *STATUS OF APPLICANTS*

A status is assigned to each applicant registered in the Older Worker Program which best describes his case.

A. *Active*

1. Applicant has been interviewed and is awaiting placement. Job openings are being personally investigated.
2. Applicant is working, but is seeking to be upgraded and in the opinion of the vocational counselor and project director is qualified to be upgraded.
3. Applicant has been accepted for MDTA training or specific employment, and has not yet started.
4. In every instance where follow-up discloses a termination, the applicant becomes active. Contact is made by telephone or letter to ascertain his reason for termination and his interest in future employment.

B. *Inactive*

1. Applicant wishes to postpone employment for a short period of time (not longer than three weeks).
2. Applicant is obtaining a medical release before placement is possible.
3. Applicant has been referred and must receive an evaluation before placement is possible.

C. *Direct Placement*

1. Applicant is referred to a job opening by the vocational counselor, accepts the job and starts to work.
2. Applicant is accepted for MDTA course and begins the course.

D. *Indirect Placement*

1. Applicant who completed application for the Older Worker Program is counseled and afterwards finds a

job through his own efforts — not referred by the
Older Worker Program vocational counselor
(motivation).

E. *Case Closed*

1. Any "hard core" applicant who is evaluated by
Social Services as unemployable, or will not involve
himself in a rehabilitative program.

2. An applicant who is unable to accept employment
due to a physical or mental disability as specified in
a medical evaluation.

3. Applicant fails to respond to two requests either by
telephone or letter that he contact the Center to
indicate his interest in employment, or applicant
agrees to an interview but fails to come in on two
occasions without notifying the Center.

4. Applicant informs the Older Worker Program that
he or she is not interested in employment.

5. Applicant restricts himself to a field of employment
or specific job requirements which are unrealistic.

VII. *FOLLOW-UP PROCEDURE*

The procedure to be taken by the Older Worker staff in
completing the follow-up of an applicant varies with the
status of the applicant.

A. *Direct Placements*

1. Follow-up is made with the employer on a one,
three, and six-month basis.

2. At this time, the employer is asked a series of
questions pertaining to the applicant, and the
completed questionnaire is given to the executive
secretary.

3. If the applicant is an alcoholic ("hard core"), the
counselor will also contact the agency or
rehabilitative program in which he is involved to
discuss the applicant's performance on the job,
attendance at meetings or interviews, and his
progress in rehabilitation.

B. *Terminations*

1. In the event of a termination, contact is made with

both the employer and the employee. The completed Employer and Employee Questionnaires are given to the executive secretary to be placed in the applicant's folder.

2. The applicant's status is changed to active.

3. The applicant is asked to notify the Center if he is interested in finding employment.

C. *Inactive*

1. All applicants will be contacted on a bi-monthly basis.

VIII. *"HARD CORE" CLASSIFICATION*

An applicant is classified as "hard core" if he possesses one or more of the following characteristics:

A. Alcoholism

B. Physical Disability

C. Mental Disability

D. Emotional Disability

E. Questionable Employability

1. unmotivated

2. unrealistic restrictions

3. poor work history (lack of experience)

4. police record

5. language barrier

6. lack of education

IX. *REFERRAL PROCEDURE*

A. When the applicant indicates a need for referral, the initial interviewer or the vocational counselor will make a determination and will process the referral.

B. The known alcoholic will be referred in every instance to Social Services.

C. If the applicant's work record discloses two or more terminations within a three-month period, the vocational counselor will automatically discuss the case with the program director to determine the need for a referral.

D. When appropriate, referrals will be made to an outside agency, i.e., Social Security, Welfare, Veterans' Administration, etc.

X. *REFERRAL PROCEDURE FOR THE ALCOHOLIC*

A. The known alcoholic, in every instance, is referred to Social Services for evaluation before placement action is instituted by the Older Worker Program. If the Social Services evaluation indicates that the applicant is employable, the applicant is then advised by the Older Worker staff that he must:

1. Affiliate himself with an agency or program, i.e., Alcoholics Anonymous or a hospital clinic. The alcoholic applicant who is termed "employable" by Social Services is, at the same time, referred by Social Services to an agency which will be of benefit to him; and,

2. Agree to this mandatory requirement before job placement can be effected and his attendance at the above-named institution or organization must be regular, not periodic at his convenience.

B. When the alcoholic is referred to the Older Worker Program by an outside agency, hospital, clinic or otherwise, this agency will be advised that a medical evaluation must be furnished. The vocational counselor will ask the alcoholic applicant referred by other agencies for an authorization for release of information from the referring agency, clinic or institution.

C. The Older Worker vocational counselor, in every instance, will acquaint the prospective employer as to the background of the applicant.

D. The alcoholic applicant termed "employable" by Social Services who engages in a program as heretofore described, will often be advised that a job of a temporary nature will be effected that may or may not be commensurate with his abilities only for the purpose of his establishing a work record. This factor, coupled with the aspect of making mandatory the applicant's acceptance of clinical and/or other assistance, follows closely the theory advanced by industry wherein the person's job is threatened unless he agrees to take part in a program that will be of benefit to him.

XI. *RECORD KEEPING*
   A. The following forms on applicants will be found in folders and kept in the central office file:
      1. Application Form
      2. Work History Form
      3. Evaluation Form
      4. MT-101 Form
      5. Health Questionnaire
      6. Reference Check Form
      7. Test Results
   B. A separate file will show each status and category and skill level of the applicant so that at any given time, an exact account may be made of:

      Status
      1. active
      2. inactive
      3. direct placement
      4. indirect placement
      5. case closed

      Hard Core
      1. alcoholic
      2. physical disability
      3. mental disability
      4. emotional problems
      5. questionable employability
         a. unmotivated
         b. unrealistic restrictions
         c. poor work history
         d. police record
         e. language barrier
         f. lack of education

   C. Employer Inquiry Form is used to obtain specific job information from employer.
   D. Placement Follow-up — the vocational counselor will make a notation on interview form as to the time of the interview, and will contact employer on that date to ascertain whether the applicant has been hired.
   E. As a result of this call, an entry is made in applicant's folder and in the card file on applicant category.
   F. The follow-up returns, described in administrative section, are given to the secretary and proper entry is made in applicant's folder and on index card.
   G. Applicant placed more than one time — each

placement is considered a separate placement for record keeping purposes.

H. Referrals — vocational counselor will complete referral form and will immediately notify executive secretary and forward said referral form to proper service. Secretary will enter referral in referral card file and note date for contact. Form goes into applicant's folder after referral service evaluates the applicant.

I. A weekly compilation will be made by the executive secretary showing number of applicants in each category.

XII. *PROCEDURE FOR JOB LISTING*

A. Each opening phoned into the Center will be recorded on the Employer Inquiry Form. All possible data on the job will be entered and a number placed in the upper left-hand corner. Information from the questionnaire will be transcribed to the master sheets of jobs available (male or female) and the corresponding job number entered.

B. Each morning, local papers will be studied for openings with an eye toward particular clients. All possibilities will be checked by phone and entries will be made in the manner described above.

C. Every two weeks, the master sheet will be reviewed and jobs that were entered over 30 days ago will be deleted.

D. Before suggesting job openings to client, each job, regardless of date of entry, will be checked by phone to determine availability.

XIII. *POLICY*

The policy of the Older Worker Program and any changes, innovations or substitutions thereof will be formulated by the director. Before affecting changes in policy, same will be discussed with the staff.

The policy of the Older Worker Program will conform strictly to the mandate of the Older Worker contract (#32-23-66-92).

Record keeping procedures for carrying out the policy will be the responsibility of the director in conjunction with the staff members designed by him. Any changes in the record keeping will be discussed with all staff members.

CHAPTER 5

THE COLLEGE PARK
GEORGIA PROGRAM

SUE HECHT

How the Program was Developed
Funding Sources
Organizational Structure
Staffing and Administration
Services Provided
Problems Encountered
Constitution

HOW THE PROGRAM WAS DEVELOPED

THE College Park Recreation Department Young at Heart's Club was organized in October of 1972. The program was developed on two-folds:

1. Being a municipal Recreation Department with the goal of providing citizens of all ages of College Park a well rounded program of recreational opportunities throughout the year, the Department thought it necessary to include the elderly citizens of College Park in its total program.

2. The College Park Housing Authority Urban Renewal project, included duplex living units for the elderly of College Park, who qualified to live in Urban Renewal. The project built a club house amid the duplexes, to provide some sort of Recreation for the occupants. The Director of the Housing Authority contacted the Recreation Department asking for assistance in setting up a program. The Housing Authorities offered the club house and the use of limited financial help.

Informing the elderly community of a Senior Citizen program began with distribution of a flyer. This information sheet, sought to find those who were interested and what their interests were, it was sent to local Senior Citizen church members, and to the Housing Authority list of Senior Citizens in the project. News paper releases were sent to the four local papers and the program was included in the Recreation Department brochure of activities.

An organizational meeting date was set up to get the show on the road. A presentation by the Director of the Recreation Department explained the role of the Recreation Department and Housing Authority in organizing the program. A fair representation of about twenty-five were present at this question and answer session. A date was set to have a pot-luck luncheon and further planning for the club.

FUNDING SOURCES

Four sources of funding are used by the club.

1. The Recreation Department budget includes a portion for the Senior Citizens.

2. The Housing Authority furnished the club house with kitchen supplies and games and continues to replenish necessary items.

3. A fee of $1.00 per year is collected from each member and is kept in a special checking account by the Treasurer.

4. Donations from interested civic groups and individuals contribute to the funding.

ORGANIZATIONAL STRUCTURE

The Recreation Department furnishes the club with a staff member, advising and contribution ideas to the members.

A President, Vice-President, Secretary, and Treasurer are elected once a year by the members and they take charge of the business and planning aspect of the group as well as the meetings. Committee chairman and workers are also an important part of the structure. A constitution was written and it serves as a guideline for the officers.

STAFFING AND ADMINISTRATION

The Recreation Department staff member is a Recreation

Center Director. She works with the club whenever they meet and is readily available for further assistance. Additional Recreation staff personnel help out when needed.

The Director of the Recreation Department serves in the official administrative position.

SERVICES PROVIDED

The Club chose to meet bi-monthly on the first and third Thursday of each month. Originally the first meeting was set aside for business while the second was the Recreational meeting. Finding the business meeting did not interest many members, we now have two Recreational meetings a month. Additional special activities will provide a third meeting date a month. The club officers meet at the end of each month to plan the up coming meetings. They also discuss additional business and it is presented at the meetings. The Recreation Department provides the assistance of their staff and also vehicles for transportation. Members are not confined to the Urban Renewal project and some live a distance away. The vehicles are used to provide transportation to the meetings.

Activities available for members are varied, due to both their interest and mobility. Arts and crafts workshops are held once a month, with an interested instructor volunteering her time. Singing is a popular activity enjoyed greatly through the donation of a piano for the building. Pot luck luncheons with a program following are a favorite by all. Bingo parties are very popular with the members bringing a small gift to be given as prizes. Guest speakers of many backgrounds and special entertainment are also a hit! Holiday parties are always fun. The Atlanta Public Library offers free films for Senior Citizen and the club has taken advantage of this service. Trips are indeed a highlight of the activities. Most of the trips are local, since the Atlanta area offers such a variety of attractions. However, an overnight trip to either Nashville, Tennessee or Charleston, South Carolina is in plans for the future.

A meeting reminder sheet is sent at the end of each month informing the members of upcoming events. This is a service of the Recreation Department.

Service projects in local hospitals and Nursing Homes are planned as a future project.

PROBLEMS ENCOUNTERED

Participation and maintaining interest among the members is a problem. An attempt has been made to evaluate the activities in order to understand the reason for the lack of interest. The problem we face, is a fear on the part of the elderly committing themselves to the organization and a feeling of non-involvement.

Of course there are a handful of members who keep the club together and they are trying by word of mouth to sustain interest.

Financially the Young at Heart's are well endowed and activity suggestions are plentiful. Currently the club has a membership of forty on the books with an average participation of fifteen.

Further directions are a membership campaign drive and continued enjoyed activities.

CONSTITUTION

Article I

Name

The name of this organization shall be the YOUNG AT HEARTS' CLUB and it shall be under the auspices of the College Park Recreation Department of the City of College Park, Georgia.

Article II

Purpose of the Club

The purpose of the "Young at Hearts' Club" shall be:
1. To develop new friendships and cooperation among its members.
2. To develop new experiences both cultural and recreational among its members.

3. To play together, work together, and to share experiences, hobbies, and memories with one another.
4. To help brighten the lives of senior citizens.
5. To assist the rest of the community with service projects and other programs.

Article III

Membership

Membership in the "Young at Hearts' Club" shall be open to all senior citizens, who are retired and/or fifty-five years or over. A complete roster of membership shall be maintained.

Article IV

Officers

Section 1. The officers shall be President, Vice-President, Secretary and Treasurer.

Section 2. The President shall act as presiding officer at regular and special meetings: call meetings of the organization: appoint standing committees: fill vacancies in office with the approval of the Executive Board: and direct the activities of the organization in accordance with the constitution.

Section 3. The Vice-President shall serve as presiding officer in the absence of the President and in the event of the resignation or death of the President. He or she shall serve as chairman of the Program Committee and shall perform such duties as the President or the Executive Board shall assign him.

Section 4. The Secretary shall keep a record of the minutes of the Executive Board and regular meetings. He or she shall handle all correspondence as directed by the President or the membership.

Section 5. The Treasurer shall collect any dues or assessments that may be made and keep a record of all collections and expenditures.

Section 6. The officers shall be elected during the election period as stated in Article VII sec. 2, and shall serve for a term of one year. No officer shall serve in each office for more than two consecutive terms.

Section 7. In order to be eligible to hold office, a member must be a member in good standing.

Section 8. Any expenditure of the Clubs' funds in excess of $10.00 must be approved by the Executive Board.

Article V

Boards & Committees

Section 1. The Executive Board shall consist of the past President, the President, the Vice-President, the Secretary, the Treasurer, and a member appointed by the Department of Recreation.

Section 2. The Executive Board shall have the authority to act in matters requiring immediate decision and action.

Section 3. The following standing committees shall be appointed:

> Program
> Membership
> Trips and Excursions
> Nominating
> Greeting

Section 4. Program Committee — Duties

a. To prepare a program of social and recreational events for the entire year.

b. To find old interests and develop new interests among members in the areas of Arts and Crafts, Hobbies, Music, Dance, Games, and other Recreational activities.

c. To arrange for programs in these areas at the meetings.

d. To plan programs for each social meeting and each feature function such as Mother's Day, Father's Day, Christmas, etc.

e. To help the members share their experience in the above areas with each other.

f. Invite leaders and other persons with interests in these areas to participate in the Clubs' activities.

g. Be responsible for all equipment used in Clubs activities — games, selection of music, etc.

Section 5. Membership Committee — Duties

a. To inform and interest the senior citizens of our community in the club and get them to join.

b. Be in charge of attendance.

Section 6. Nominating Committee — Duties

a. The President shall appoint a nominating committee of five (5) members in October of each year and said committee shall prepare a slate of two names for each elective office. Additional nominations may be made from the floor. At the regular business meeting in November at which time the nominations will be closed.

b. Prepare the ballots for the election.

c. Tally the votes and announce the results.

d. Plan the program for installation of officers.

Section 7. Greeting Committee — Duties

a. Remember members who are ill or in sorrow.

b. Brighten the lives of senior citizens who are shut in (whether members or not).

c. To prepare a Devotional session on the start of each meeting.

d. Welcome new members and visitors and serve as reception committee at all functions of the club.

Section 8. Field Trips and Excursions Committee — Duties

a. Make all arrangements for field trips and excursions.

b. Include in these arrangements the following:
   1. Transportation
   2. Luncheon reservations
   3. Site
   4. Picnics as well as restaurant lunches, Industrial and commercial sites, etc.

c. Arrange signing up procedures for trips by members.

d. The Treasurer shall serve as a member on this committee.

e. The President shall appoint a special committee for out-of-town trips.

Section 9. Ad hoc Committees — Formation

a. To be appointed by the President for specific duties as needed by the club.

Article VI

Meetings

Meetings shall be held on the first and third Wednesday of each month; the regular business meeting on the first and social recreation on the third Wednesday.

Article VII

Election of Officers

Section 1. Election of officers shall be by secret ballot.

Section 2. Election of officers will be held at a daytime meeting on the date of the first regular business meeting in December. Time and place to be announced.

Section 3. The nominating Committee shall be in full charge of the elections.

Section 4. New officers shall be installed into office at the first regular business meeting in January.

Article VIII

Eligible to Vote

Section 1. In order to be eligible to vote a member must be in good standing.

Section 2. A member in good standing is one who has his or her dues paid up and has attended 50% of the meetings throughout the past year.

Article IX

Membership Dues

Section 1. The dues of this club should be one dollar per annum, payable in January of each year; new members are to pay when they join.

Section 2. Visitors who wish to join the Club are welcome to take part in any phase of the Club's program, but only members will be accepted on field trips.

Article X

Amendments

Amendments may be made to the Constitution by a majority vote when a quorum is present at a regular business meeeting. Fifty percent of the membership shall constitute a quorum.

CHAPTER 6

JOHN F. KENNEDY
FAMILY SERVICE CENTER

John T. Gardiner

How the Program Was Developed
Funding Sources
Organizational Structure
Staffing and Administration
Services Provided
Description of Senior Services
Future Directions

HOW THE PROGRAM WAS DEVELOPED

THE Kennedy Center was established in 1964 as the first and only community social service agency in Charlestown, a neighborhood in Boston. The Kennedy Center was funded by the Ford Foundation as a multi-service center in anticipation of the physical and social trauma expected in connection with a massive urban renewal program in the community, involving family dislocation and associated problems. Among those most seriously affected by these developments was the elderly population which has always comprised a relatively large and poor segment of the community. Typical of the social service programs to assist the elderly was a major effort to address the problems of the aging worker. From these beginnings, the Senior Service activities developed into a distinct programmatic entity, which is more fully described below.

FUNDING SOURCES

The Kennedy Center, as has been indicated above, was

originally funded by Ford Foundation to provide multiple social services including elderly services. After three years of Ford Foundation funding, the Senior Services Program was funded from two principal sources; namely, the Office of Economic Opportunity (OEO), and United Community Services (UCS). This funding pattern has existed to the present. With the prospective termination of OEO funding, greater emphasis must be placed upon UCS and alternative funding sources in the future.

ORGANIZATIONAL STRUCTURE

A copy of the organization chart of the Kennedy Center is attached for your review. Two critical points should be made with reference to it. First is the critical role of the community elected Board of Directors which makes the Kennedy Center a uniquely effective and representative organization of the community. And, secondly, the emphasis as reflected in the Program Integration Committee, to coordinate the several program areas into an interactive multi-service delivery system, from which families have access to comprehensive services regardless of their point of entry into the organization. These two emphases must be considered to appreciate the organizational framework and context in which the Senior Services Program operates.

STAFFING AND ADMINISTRATION

The program is staffed with a full-time director and three part-time neighborhood workers. Also included on the staff is a part-time secretary and a part-time custodian for program facilities. Program coordination is the responsibility of the program director, while the director and the neighborhood workers are all involved in provision of services and supervision of responsibilities.

This program staff is supported by the other program and administrative staff described on the organization chart referred to above.

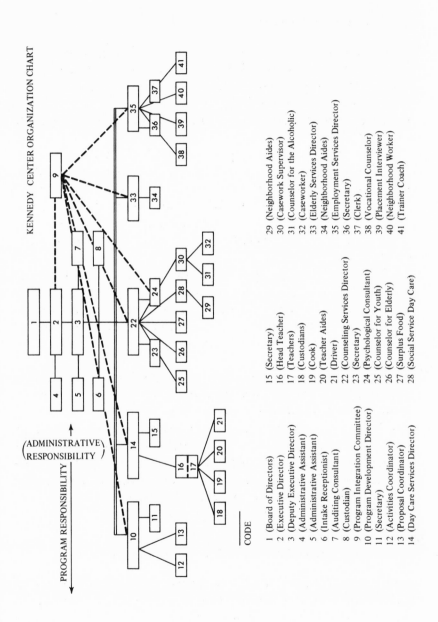

KENNEDY CENTER ORGANIZATION CHART

PROGRAM RESPONSIBILITY

(ADMINISTRATIVE RESPONSIBILITY)

CODE

1 (Board of Directors)
2 (Executive Director)
3 (Deputy Executive Director)
4 (Administrative Assistant)
5 (Administrative Assistant)
6 (Intake Receptionist)
7 (Auditing Consultant)
8 (Custodian)
9 (Program Integration Committee)
10 (Program Development Director)
11 (Secretary)
12 (Activities Coordinator)
13 (Proposal Coordinator)
14 (Day Care Services Director)

15 (Secretary)
16 (Head Teacher)
17 (Teachers)
18 (Custodians)
19 (Cook)
20 (Teacher Aides)
21 (Driver)
22 (Counseling Services Director)
23 (Secretary)
24 (Psychological Consultant)
25 (Counselor for Youth)
26 (Counselor for Elderly)
27 (Surplus Food)
28 (Social Service Day Care)

29 (Neighborhood Aides)
30 (Casework Supervisor)
31 (Counselor for the Alcoholic)
32 (Caseworker)
33 (Elderly Services Director)
34 (Neighborhood Aides)
35 (Employment Services Director)
36 (Secretary)
37 (Clerk)
38 (Vocational Counselor)
39 (Placement Interviewer)
40 (Neighborhood Worker)
41 (Trainer Coach)

SERVICES PROVIDED

Need for Senior Services

The Senior Services Program is designed to provide for the basic social needs of elderly people in the Charlestown community. Its emphasis is thus twofold:
— Providing social services; and,
— In a manner appropriate to the needs and sensibilities of the elderly.

Of the total Charlestown population of 15,000 as reported in the 1970 census, approximately 2,500 persons are sixty years of age or over. Of these, it is estimated that 75 percent have incomes in the poverty level. Many are further afflicted with a variety of physical and/or psychological disabilities, which contribute to a serious degree of social isolation. Most are female, and almost all are white.

Of the total elderly population, approximately 500 live in the public Housing Project, with almost 100 more living in the recently completed elderly housing units in another section of the community. The remainder live in individual private residences or small multiple unit dwellings throughout the community. Many live alone.

Of the 2,500 persons in the elderly population in Charlestown, approximately 1,200 are involved in the Senior Services Program of the Kennedy Center. By design of our outreach program, these people tend to be those who have no other means of assistance from other sources, particularly family sources. For this reason, we believe the most seriously affected segment of the elderly population is being reached; but, even to that extent, limited resources preclude providing truly comprehensive services or extending services to additional people in need.

DESCRIPTION OF SENIOR SERVICES

The primary function of this program is to provide social aid and personal services to any resident of Charlestown, sixty years of age or over. Activities center around an elderly lounge, located at 55 Bunker Hill Street, which is open to the elderly Monday through Friday, 12 noon to 4 p.m. Regularly scheduled activities include:

— Escorting persons to and from hospital or clinic visits of a routine or an emergency nature.
— Visiting the sick and shut-ins.
— Generating an interest in community affairs through educational trips, guest speakers, conferences on elderly affairs.
— Conducting a weekly group food shopping program for the elderly.
— Planning and supervising a variety of entertaining field trips and community activities, including weekly bingo games, movies, birthday parties and fun days.
— Preparing hot meals for the elderly from surplus food commodities.
— Helping elderly with problems of housing or relocation.
— Providing sympathetic attention to all aspects of the problems of the elderly.
— Informing the elderly of the employment and counseling services offered through other departments of the Kennedy Center and insuring that necessary referrals are made.
— Check cashing for shut-ins and payment of bills including rent, electricity, gas, etc.
— Shopping on an emergency basis.
— Taking prescriptions to the pharmacy and arranging for large print on prescription labels, making sure that medicine is taken as directed.
— Referrals to other agencies as appropriate including homemaker services, the Bunker Hill Health Center, Visiting Nurse Association, and other records of referrals and follow-up are maintained.
— An annual free Thanksgiving Dinner attended by the elderly in the community and representatives of community social and political agencies, which has become a notable community gathering.

In addition to these activities, the Elderly Lounge is opened Monday to Friday, 1 p.m. to 4 p.m. with the following schedule of

weekly events under the supervision of at least one staff member:
— Monday, Wednesday, and Friday: Fun days for recreational activities of various kinds.
— Tuesday: Knitting, crocheting and rug making with lessons given.
— Thursday: Group shopping day with transportation provided.

Wherever possible, these activities are extended to the shut-ins as well. Every month, a birthday party is given and cards are given to each individual whose birthday falls in that month, including shut-ins.

FUTURE DIRECTIONS

The future of the Senior Services Program will depend to a great extent upon the source of future funding for elderly activities. In an effort to expand potential funding sources for the elderly, various representative of the Kennedy Center sit as members of Elderly Councils at the state and city level. From this participation has come a greater sense of future viability and direction in this program area, particularly with the reorganization of the State Office of Elder Affairs which will coordinate funding for the elderly. The organizational and programmatic model for service delivery under the state plan is the Home Care Corporation. Through this concept, the Kennedy Center can consolidate and expand its existing elderly services. For your review, the following is a description of the basic program model as envisioned by the State Office of Elder Affairs:

An array of basic services will be provided in *all* Home Care Programs, while supplementary services may be provided by Programs in some areas to serve special needs. The basic services described below are expected to be performed in every Home Care Program.

Standards for these programs are suggested in two ways: First, the list of basic services which follows suggests a standard of service in general terms for each Home Care Program. Second, a set of standards in each basic service functional area will be established. It is expected that these standards will be refined and modified by the Office of Elder Affairs as the programs evolve.

Basic Services

Basic services consist of a minimum of seven services:

1. Case finding information and referral and follow-up services. This service will make contact with eligible people in the Home Care Program area and provide basic information about individuals so that additional services may be provided as necessary. This includes using existing identified populations as well as identifying populations not associated with existing programs.

   This service will provide information, referral and follow-up necessary to insure the delivery of available services to participants in the Home Care Program. This is a personal contact service attached to an information and control system which will insure that services are delivered.

2. Homemaker and chore services

   This service will provide such services as personal and food shopping, escort service, check cashing and bill paying, errands, light housekeeping, yard chores, minor repairs and meal preparation as necessary. In short, this service sustains activities necessary to daily life.

3. Housing services

   This service will assess the adequacy of housing arrangements and make such alternative arrangements as necessary to provide an adequate standard of housing, including household safety.

   Activities which may support this service include the use of foster care resources in the area, the establishment of priority arrangements with local housing authorities or private landlords for Home Care Program participants, and the development of housing units for use by the Home Care Program.

4. Health maintenance and nutrition services

   The health service will maintain the physical and emotional well being of participants, and will restore physical and mental health through treatment and rehabilitation. This service will provide direct medical care in homes and in central facilities where appropriate and insure accessibility of existing medical services. It is strongly suggested that the homemaker-home health aide services be developed in conjunction with each other so as to eliminate the distinction and to maximize third party payments for each. Home care agencies should plan on applying for home health agency status. This service will provide a system for identifying and fulfilling the nutritional needs of participants. This may require the provision of a central meals service and emergency meals-on-wheels service, including an emphasis on nutritional and consumer education.

In Region VI the Executive Office or Elder Affairs would like to explore the feasibility of using an economic development approach to nutrition planning.

5. Legal services

This service assures access to legal counsel as necessary, particularly for protective services. Protective services include services required when the individual is no longer able to effectively make decisions for himself, and action is necessary for his personal well being.

6. Transportation services

This service assures the provision of transportation by automobile or some other vehicle for medical, sustaining life, and social needs of participants. Applicants should explore the potential of already existing transportation services and use of vehicles owned by major institutions such as school departments, hospitals and other agencies.

7. Emergency service

This service assures access by telephone to emergency agencies on an as-needed basis beyond the regular times at which organizations in the Home Care Program usually function.

It should be noted that the above services may be performed in a variety of ways. An agency may provide more or less than one of the above services. However, through one organizational relationship or another, all of the above services must be performed by each Home Care Program.

Supplementary Services

These services are seen to be useful, and indeed, may be

judged to be basic services in some Home Care Program, but are not required in general. Funding for some supplementary components may depend upon availability of adequate resources.

1. A variety of groups are neglected and particularly need well developed services due to their positions in the larger culture. Special services, such as indigenous staff with cultural and language sensitivity and skills, may be developed to make the basic service program effective.
2. Services to blind adults.
3. Service to handicapped adults.
4. Educational services.
5. Employment services.
6. Service opportunity programs.
7. Recreation
   Programs for entertainment and diversion such as bus trips, film showing, sports participation and watching may be included in the Home Care Program.
8. Religious contacts
   The Home Care Program may arrange with individual clergymen and groups of clergymen to ask them to visit Home Care Program participants if the Home Care Program participants so request.
9. Special services for locally determined needs
   Home Care Programs may develop other services which cater to special needs of interests identified by various participants as the Program develops.

We see this framework as a viable future direction for the Kennedy Center's Senior Services Program.

CHAPTER 7

SENIOR CITIZENS PROGRAM OF SAVANNAH-CHATHAM COUNTY, GEORGIA

ANNE R. SULLIVAN

OUR organization is a private non-profit agency incorporated in January 1960 as Senior Citizens-Savannah-Chatham County. It was the outgrowth of the dedicated group of people who knew the needs of the older citizens in Savannah and wanted to do something to help them. Before they were accepted as part of United Community Services, they solicited funds through individual contributions and began to serve the elderly in Savannah.

The program demonstrated its worth early and now enjoys a board base of Community support. Funding comes from a variety of sources, membership dues ($2.00 a year for those who can afford it), United Community Services, City and County, Title III from the State Commission on Aging, Private Donations, Clubs, local churches, Banks, Sororities and Model Cities Supplemental Funds replacing a cut-back on Title XVI. Membership consists of about 66 2/3 percent of the total Senior Citizens population of Savannah, some 10,500 persons over 60 years old. Members have increased threefold in the past six years. Senior Citizens is a service oriented agency open to anyone over 60, with no regard to race, color or creed. From the beginning all our services were integrated.

The few citizens who founded the agency were able to persuade the City of Savannah to begin a special recreation program for the elderly. These groups were known as Golden Age Clubs. The primary purpose of these clubs was to provide social and recreational outlets for older persons. The first Golden Age Center was started at the Jewish Educational Alliance under the auspices of the Council of Jewish Women. Volunteers taught crafts. Other churches began to be concerned with the elderly persons in their parishes and sponsored gatherings for Senior Citizens. Depending on volunteers with no real leader was unsatisfactory so the City Recreation Department provided "Leaders" for 10 centers — in public housing projects and later in churches. When the City took over operation of the Golden Age Clubs the founding group assumed the Advocacy Role for Senior Citizens in the Community and concentrated on services to Senior Citizens.

An Information and Referral Center was set up to inform Senior Citizens of community resources available to them. These resources in the beginning were limited but they grew as the agency began to expand services and meet needs. An outlet for the handmade articles was provided at the Center. The sale of these articles provides a supplement to the meagre incomes of the elderly. The handiwork is not available anywhere else. Some crafts are almost extinct.

Savannah is an historic city steeped in tradition. Tourists from other parts of the country delight in finding such things as: pine needle baskets, handmade tatting, caning, Mammy Dolls, baby clothes with feather stitching, sweaters, afghans, aprons, quilts in many patterns, pot holders, rugs, bonnets and other articles. This can be done easily in any community featuring articles typical of the place.

The Board got busy and appealed to the citizens of the community to help. The membership card began to entitle Senior Citizens to discounts on drugs, on dry cleaning, on eyeglasses, ball games and free movies on certain mornings. Later the transit authority included bus tokens on the list. Banks offer free checking accounts.

Two elderly ladies were provided employment and the community was offered an alteration service with the addition of a sewing room. Simple alterations, blanket binding and quilting are available. The service is reasonable, convenient and very popular.

Some perceptive Board member saw the need for pallets for local industries. They could be relatively easily constructed and there was a ready market for the product. From a very small beginning with hand saws this idea has grown under the capable guidance of an aggressive Board President, Mr. H. C. Morrison, to a $150,000 business. It gives employment to some 25 elderly men who might otherwise feel completely useless.

Someone saw waste from a trailer manufacturer, nuts, screws and bolts being hauled away to the dump. It occured to him that it could be salvaged and save the company money. Of course the management bought the idea. Two elderly gentlemen with severe heart damage sit at a table several hours a day sorting the waste and sell it back to Great Dane Trailer Company. They have a meaningful role and are proud of their work. You should talk with them! A workshop like this can flourish in any community with just a little vision. There are endless possibilities.

I cannot emphasize too much the importance of sincere interest in the problems of the elderly for those working in a program for Senior Citizens. The accomplishments of the small dedicated group of Founders of Senior Citizens-Savannah-Chatham County, Inc. has accomplished miracles. Special accolades should go to: Mr. Morrison (mentioned above), Mrs. David Byck, Mr. Hunter Leaf, Mrs. Jeannette Hackett (now deceased), Mr. William Benton and Mr. Ted Earle. Their continued interest and community contacts over the years have been invaluable.

In 1965 the need for a Social Services Program became apparent and a Social Worker was added to the small staff. The Board was conservative in their thinking. Their already noteworthy accomplishments have been achieved on a "shoe string." They were reluctant to seek Federal funding but the close relationship with the Georgia Commission on Aging brought the consideration to the realm of possibility. A small grant of Title III, Administration on Aging funds, was made for a Friendly Visitors Program.

It was at this point that the programs began to take shape. We were able to recruit but more importantly to train our volunteers by offering transportation to selected Senior Citizens who could not afford to use their own cars or public transportation without subsidy. The Friendly Visitors began to meet a need but probably just as significantly the program made the older volunteers feel needed. So immediately our program filled a dual purpose.

Mrs. Elsie Alvis, then Director of the State Commission on Aging, and her staff gave invaluable professional counsel in addition to providing necessary funds. The insistence on adequate records and training volunteers has been most helpful. The growth of our program is indicated by a comparison of a few figures! The caseload in January 1966 was 30 and in June 1968 it was 150! We stressed quality in our volunteers rather than increasing numbers. The services our volunteers give are numerous and their efforts untiring. By familiarizing the volunteers with the community resources through the use of agency professionals in our training programs they became sensitive to individual needs. Group meetings and discussion of mutual problems are good tools for learning resources.

Our determined, energetic Mrs. Byck was impressed with a very expensive and sophisticated Meals on Wheels Program in the North. First dreams for the program had to be abandoned because such an elaborate program could not be supported on a continuing basis. But this little lady is never discouraged and she pressed on with the idea despite lack of enthusiasm from her associates. Mrs. Byck talked the Meals on Wheels Program to every organization that would listen and the response was tremendous. She came up with an exceptional group of young women from the Whitfield Methodist Church who agreed to deliver the T.V. dinners regularly. The project was funded through an expansion of our Title III grant in May 1967. We purchased a freezer and bought a variety of Morton T.V. Dinners wholesale. We expected to serve 40 people during the first year. At the present time we are serving 60 individuals 3 meals a week. From May through December 1967 eight wonderful volunteers delivered 3890 T.V. dinners to shut-ins without a hitch. They have never failed to show up at the appointed time and have always sent a substitute when they could not come. The program runs smoothly with a minimum of problems and the potential for continued growth is limited only by finances. Feeding elderly poor unable to prepare food for themselves is an appealing cause in any community.

To my knowledge the Friendly Visitors and Meals on Wheels Programs are the only projects that gained such wide community support to continue to operate when federal funding terminated.

In 1969 it seemed that Savannah might qualify for a Model Cities Grant. We attended many planning meetings and plugged for our Senior Citizens' needs to be met. Our previous experience on a comparatively small scale gave us the knowhow to seek means to establish more coordinated comprehensive services to the elderly in Savannah.

We submitted a proposal which was accepted and in October 1970 our Staff went to work on the new project. Mrs. Dorothy B. Taylor, Mrs. Sally L. Waters and myself were the beginning team. Savannah Model Cities was one of the few projects in the nation which designed a program exclusively for services to Senior Citizens.

The grant for the Model Cities Program, limited to a designated area and completely Federally funded, is administered by the Board of the private parent agency and the Model Cities City Demonstration Agency is guided by the Senior Citizens Council of United Community Services comprised of the executives of every agency in Savannah offering service to Seniors, 7 volunteers and 3 persons from the staff of the United Community Services. Technical assistance is provided from the now Office on Aging-Georgia Department of Human Resources, the National Council on Aging, the local Health Department, National Council of Homemakers-Home Health Aides and others.

Model Cities Supplemental funds make it possible for us to provide services to Senior Citizens that were only dreams before.

I honestly believe that the advent of the Model Cities Senior Citizens Program has generated improved services to the elderly in our community that otherwise might have taken years to develop. Economic Opportunity Authority is more concerned, the Department of Family and Childrens Services are more active, Legal Aid is more involved and the entire community is more aware of the needs of Senior Citizens. Surely the two High Rises for the elderly here are credited to at least some extent to efforts on the part of Senior Citizens-Savannah-Chatham County, Inc.

At the beginning of the Model Cities Program we pledged to give employment to poverty level persons within the Model Neighborhood *at least* 50 years or older. The mean age of our outreach workers is 59 years. We never will make a wiser decision. These people have proved reliable, sensitive and untiring in their efforts to provide services to their less fortunate peers. There has been practically no staff turnover since the program began.

After recruiting workers from the Model Neighborhood, many of whom were limited economically and academically, we set about the task of training our workers. There was tremendous agency response to provide professionals to appraise our workers of existing resources available to Senior Citizens. Some who assisted early were: Department of Family and Childrens Services, Old Age Assistance and Food Stamp Supervisors, the Director of Social Services-Memorial Hospital, the Director of our local Social Security Office, a Public Health Nurse, Mrs. Naomi Edwards, then liaison to Model Cities, Georgia Commission on Aging, a Minister to explain the spiritual needs of the elderly and the Director of Model Cities. In addition to training by agency professionals, Mrs. Dorothy B. Taylor (then Social Services Supervisor-now Assistant Director) did a fine job of teaching personal grooming and hygiene. The Manual for Training National Council Homemakers-Home Health Aids was utilized to teach the Homemakers. Each worker has an American Red Cross First Aid certificate. Consumer courses were added. Good training is an integral part of any program. During the first year of operation Mr. Braxton Warner, Regional Representative, National Council on Aging and the Staff of the State Office on Aging maintained a close working relationship, keeping us informed on developments in the field. Mrs. Marie Maguire, Elderly Affairs Specialist for Department of Housing and Urban Development visited us and gave us advice to help the agency accomplish our mission.

Our first step in starting the work in Model Cities was to conduct a house to house survey in the neighborhoods, locate the lonely isolated elderly and learn their needs. An evaluation is necessary for the coordinated delivery of services in the community. The out-reach workers tried to evaluate 1) the ability to complete the activities of daily living 2) health status of the Senior Citizen 3) his mental health 4) his social situation and 5) an appraisal of his economic circumstances. This survey took three months. At first the aged residents were reluctant to accept our workers because of deep seated fears and suspicions. As the gold uniforms became familiar and neighbors began to talk of benefits our caseload increased to 2000 Senior Citizens receiving some type service. We have 24 outreach workers giving a variety of services to our people.

The office staff concerns itself with Information, Referral and Follow-up Service, Supervision of Homemakers and Community Aides and Administration of the overall program, as well as close contact with the community by various means including the news media.

After two years of research at Duke University, Eric Pfieffer, M.D. has come up with a list of Geriatric Services needed for comprehensive programs for the elderly, (table pg. 161). Of the 23 services listed our agency provides 20. Our psychiatric services are minimal but we are working now with the Comprehensive Mental Health and the Georgia Regional Hospital to bridge this gap. Surrogate Services are inadequate because we do not have funds for legal consultation and Georgia laws are at present non existent. We are working to improve this situation.

Our services are designed to provide in-home care to help the elderly live independent meaningful lives out of institutions.

A Central Intake, Referral and Follow-up Unit includes initial interviews to determine eligibility for services, referral to other Model Cities projects, other community resources and follow-up to determine how the project has benefited the client.

Homemaker Services are provided to 120 clients who are unable to carry out domestic tasks because of age, infirmity, or handicap. This service consists of, but is not limited to: light housekeeping and laundry, meal preparation and planning, personal care (invalid grooming, bed care, sponge bathing and administering medicine under the direction of a Public Health Nurse).

Chore Aide Service provides elderly persons with services like homemaking, but also includes shopping, bill paying and any needed service. Chore Aides serve 1021 Seniors each month.

Day Care Service may provide a day out for a relative burdened with the constant care of a sick Senior Citizen or allows a younger family member to work or attend to personal affairs.

Meals on Wheels consists of delivery of one meal per day for five days per week to 300 homebound persons unable to cook themselves. The dinner meets 1/3 of the daily nutritional requirements of the FDA. One quart of whole milk per week, soup and gelatin to those unable to consume solids is delivered.

TABLE 1

List of Generic Services

1. Coordination of services	13. Legal consultation
2. Counseling — psychotherapy	14. Surrogate services
3. Counseling of family members	15. Transportation
4. Psychotropic drugs	16. Assistance in finding paid employment
5. Medical treatment	17. Assistance finding unpaid employment
6. Nursing services	18. Vocational rehabilitation services
7. Physical therapy services	19. Financial assistance
8. Recreational services	20. "Checking" services
9. Social interaction	21. Day care services
10. Personal care services	22. "Respite" care
11. Food services	23. Relocation and placement services
12. Hotel services	

Hot Meals are served to 75 clients in the Cultural Enrichment Program from Monday through Friday. Saleable crafts are taught and a display outlet provided.

We provide transportation to and from medical and dental facilities, to and from the project's Cultural Enrichment Center and for tours and outings.

Ambulatory devices including wheelchairs, crutches, canes, comode chairs and walkers are loaned needy Senior Citizens.

Pickup and delivery of prescriptions is offered to aid maintenance of health for 140 people a month.

Outreach workers give Advocate Services each month to 1300 Model Neighborhood residents. Medical care is often lacking. The benefits of Medicare and Medicaid are prime concerns. Workers inform residents of services available to the elderly, secure food stamps after they help them apply, secure discount cards and purchase bus tokens. To name a few other services — escort service, just combing an elderly lady's hair, writing a letter for a person with hands crippled by arthritis are requests we honor.

Elderly people are human individuals and our services are geared to individual needs rather than depersonalized as they have been in the past. Aging people need to find for themselves places in society where they have participation and fulfillment. Our Cultural Enrichment Center offers an opportunity for intimate social contacts to give the elderly a sense of belonging. They are taught crafts and enjoy educational trips to places around Savannah they never dreamed existed. One lady in her eighties lived here all her life and has never seen the beach twenty miles away.

Our Protective Services Program is just now being developed although the need for such a project has been evident for some years. "Protectives" are only 5% of the aging population. Lack of funds for proper legal consultation and psychiatric evaluation is a problem now as it was in the early stages of the other programs.

A "protective" is a person who is unable because of disordered mentality to maintain minimal standards of self care and conduct sufficient to avoid jeopardy to the health, safety, comfort or property of himself or others. Protection involves doing for a person those things which he cannot with some degree of competence do for himself. A good service involves a team approach where some or all of the team may or may not be needed in each case. The team consists of: a psychiatrist, a lawyer, a registered nurse, a social worker and the backup services deemed necessary. All Senior Citizens need one person to assist them with continuity and warm intelligent concern.

Many decisions we now make, in the absense of relatives, are without authority and unfair to our workers. Frequently we see cases where the older person is being taken advantage of but we are helpless to *legally* intercede. At present we are promoting passage of a Protective Services Bill for Senior Citizens in the State Legislature (1). With the sole exception of Medicare, in the past decade we have made little or no progress in the United States toward realistic societal solutions on a mass basis to problems arising from the normal, to-be-expected dependencies of aging. Professional social work, which should be in the vanguard in

1. Margaret Blenkner, S.D.W. The Normal Dependencies of Aging.

developing such solutions, still acts as though counseling and custodialism were major answers to the problems of growing old in America. Attempts to encourage new programs specifically geared to the aged are met with the Social Work — Work Establishment's territorial cry "duplication of service." Anyone who is not completely naive knows it never is raised in defense of clients, only budgets. No client ever compained of duplication of service. Most would welcome the opportunity to do some comparative shopping.

Presently Medicare and Old Age Assistance is not meeting the needs of our older citizens. In the U. S. most money and manpower directed specifically to the aged segment of the population are designed to remove the old from their own homes. In-home services are preferred by Senior Citizens and save your Tax Dollars. This success story can be a reality in any community in America with a small number of persons determined and dedicated to alleviate problems of Senior Citizens.

Acknowledgments:

I would like to express my gratitude for any success of the Model Cities Senior Citizens program to the following:

The City Demonstration Agency for their continued support.

The Board of Senior Citizens Savannah-Chatham County, Inc.

The Office on Aging — Georgia Department of Human Resources.

Dr. Ellen Winston, President National Council for Homemaker-Home Health Aide Services, for inspiration to continue our Homemaker Program in the face of discouraging odds.

Last but *not least* Margaret Blenkner, Ph.D. — the greatest social worker I have ever met.

CHAPTER 8

COUNTY OF HAWAII
SENIOR CITIZENS PROGRAM

BACKGROUND

THE Big Island Senior Citizens' Program was born as a result of Public Law 89-73, The Older American Act of 1965. The Act provided Federal Grant Funds under Title III to the State Commission on Aging for the development of programs directly serving the elderly.

In 1968, the Hilo Pomaikai Multi-purpose Senior Citizens Center was established under the sponsorship of the Department of Parks & Recreation after having received approval from the State Commission for Grant Funds under the Act. Together with matching funds from the County of Hawaii, the Center was funded for a period of three years, terminating in June of 1971. Due to the program's success, as evidenced by the tremendous response, the County of Hawaii fully subsidized the program and absorbed it as an integral part of its Parks & Recreation program beginning in July, 1971. Acknowledging the need for activities in the rural areas, the Parks & Recreation Department was able to establish satellite centers in North and South Hawaii in an attempt to extend services for the elderly in the outlying areas.

Since then, the Department has developed a total of 18 organized senior citizens' centers encompassing all parts of the island. At present, the Department is planning to incorporate four existing OEO senior centers located at Keaukaha, Lanakila, Honokaa and Pahala.

TRANSPORTATION

A key factor to the success of the senior citizens' program has been the funding of bus transportation services by the County of Hawaii. Early in the program's first year, the need for these services was recognized. It was ascertained that many elderly persons could not participate in the program — the prime factor being lack of transportation. Subsequently, the County of Hawaii, in October of 1969, funded the cost for bus transportation services for the Hilo area. A supplemental grant in March of 1971, by the County Council expanded transportation services to the rural areas. As a result, an increase in membership, utilization of facilities and services, and stabilization of attendance in center activities affecting the entire program has been evidenced.

At present, the County of Hawaii is funding this essential service and is continuing to transport the senior citizens to and from the program centers.

KONA PROJECT

In July of 1970, the Department submitted a project request for the Kona Regional area with plans to develop a senior citizens' program at the Yano Community Center. This project, which will serve a population of 1500-plus elderly who are basically classified in the low-income group, will cover a geographical span of approximately 37 miles from one end of the district to the other. The project was approved in June of 1971, and was funded for a period of three years. The Department has, at present, hired a Senior Activities Specialist for the area, formulated a staffing pattern, and has made contact with key community leaders. It is hoped that the project will provide for direct services to this area which is so far removed in terms of distance from the central complex in Hilo. Plans for the future call for the establishment of satellite centers similar to that as developed in East Hawaii.

OBJECTIVES

The primary objective of the senior citizens' program is to provide a program conducive to the physical, psychological, and social well-being of the participating elderly. The program attempts to satisfy these objectives through meaningful and wholesome recreational activities designed to create new opportunities in producing a new outlook in life.

Since the inception of the senior citizens' program, many positive psychological, physiological, and sociological benefits have been noted. This seems to indicate that the county is making some headway in attempting to meet the many needs of the elderly.

PROGRAM OF ACTIVITIES

The County of Hawaii's program of activities for senior citizens includes a variety of educational, recreational, and social adventures. In planning these programs, a wide range of offerings is scheduled in order to take into account the different abilities and interests of the participants. Key elements of the program are listed below:

1. Arts and Crafts
2. Games of low and high organization
3. Educational and recreational films
4. Social events, gatherings, and celebrations
5. Rhythmics and dance
6. Music
7. Guest speakers and special guests
8. Group travel
9. Nutrition and cooking
10. Flower Arranging
11. Activities of an outreach nature

Along with the regular program activities, efforts are made to utilize the services of various governmental and community agencies in providing health and related assistance.

The program is constantly reviewed and evaluated with new

activities being introduced continually in order to maintain the interest of the elderly.

Staffing to carry out the program in the County's 18 senior centers include: 1 Senior Activities Supervisor, 1 Senior Activities Specialist, 14 Contractual Center Aides, and 1 Half-time Clerk-Typist.

PHYSICAL FACILITIES

At present, most of the buildings utilized for the various senior citizens' centers are borrowed facilities. While presently serving a useful purpose, the functional qualities of these facilities leave much to be desired. Many facilities are inadequately equipped with poor lighting and no cooking facilities and are generally in dilapidated condition. A list with a brief description of the present senior citizens' centers is given below:

Center Location	Type of Facility
1. Hakalau	Old unused school classroom
2. Honomu	County gymnasium
3. Keaau	Buddhist Recreation Hall
4. Kohala	Episcopalian Church
5. Laupahoehoe	Old Tax Office
6. Naalehu	Plantation Clubhouse
7. Paauilo	Plantation Clubhouse
8. Pahoa	Old Buddhist Hall
9. Papaikou	Old Plantation Building
10. Pepeekeo	Old Buddhist Hall

In attempting to provide adequate facilities for the senior citizens, the County of Hawaii has considered a senior citizen building in the Kohala (Kamehameha Park) Parks master plan; however, funds for the center have not been appropriated.

SUMMARY

At present, the County of Hawaii is providing a meaningful, wholesome program of activities for its senior citizens. It has hired specialists to operate the program, secured facilities for its implementation, and provided the necessary transportation services. In 1971, over 1700 individuals and a duplicated total of

26,000 senior citizens participated in various segments of the program.

According to current statistics, however, a large percentage of elderly persons are yet to be reached. The County of Hawaii, in its ceaseless efforts to reach this untapped resource, is constantly striving to upgrade its program.

A great need for improved physical facilities also remains in producing a more effective program benefitting the elderly.

CHAPTER 9

SENIOR CITIZENS' CENTER, INC., TRINIDAD, COLORADO

DELPHINE LUCERO

SOURCES OF INCOME
ORGANIZATION
STAFFING
SERVICES BEING OFFERED

IN January of 1969 the first Senior Citizens' Center in the state of Colorado began operation with Title III funds of the Older Americans Act.

Several months of planning and research by the Las Animas County Department of Public Welfare prefaced the request for funds. Caseworkers from the Old Age Pension program interviewed clients and made door to door surveys. The local newspaper and radio station gave the proposed program extensive coverage. Organizations which have, as their over-all purpose, service to the elderly, local government officials, as well as all interested citizens were invited to attend "town hall" type meetings. The needs of the senior citizen were discussed and it was emphatically agreed that opportunities for senior citizens in Trinidad were extremely limited.

City and County officials committed themselves to match Title III monies with financial and in-kind service on an increasing annual basis. Following this commitment arrangements were made for a building site and the proposal was submitted to the Colorado Commission on Aging.

Upon receipt of the grant the Center began operation, became a non-profit corporation, and elected a nine-member board of directors.

As a result of the coal mine shutdown, which was Trinidad's

169

major industry, the city became an economically depressed area. The major concern, therefore, for the continued operation of the Senior Citizens' Center, since Title III funds are granted on a three year diminishing basis, was the ability of the community to support it financially. The first and most important aspect in long-term planning was for the acquisition of the building site. This would lessen the administrative expenditures, as it would eliminate monthly rental payment for the property. The administrative budget could then possibly be supplemented by an on-going item of expenditure in the City of Trinidad and Las Animas County budgets.

At the end of the third year of operation when Title III funds would no longer be available, the city and county were still not able to carry the full financial burden of the Center administration. Upon request to the Colorado Commission on Aging, funds were continued for an additional two years.

In 1970 Trinidad was declared a Model City through Title I of the Demonstration Cities and Metropolitan Development Act of 1966. By this time the Center had made a decided impact on the community. Members joined task force committees and became increasingly involved in civic affairs. The Model City Agency included the Senior Citizens' Center as one of its projects and the program has continued to operate and expand its services. This program also made it possible for the City of Trinidad to purchase the building for Senior Citizens's use.

SOURCES OF INCOME

1967 - 1971-Title III of the Older Americans Act on a
      diminishing basis
      Las Animas County on an increasing basis
      City of Trinidad on an increasing basis
      Project income
1972 - 1973-a. Model City Agency on a diminishing basis
      b. Las Animas County, increasing
      c. City of Trinidad, increasing
      d. Project income
        1. membership fees

2. private contributions
3. fund-raising activities
4. Center rental

Funding for 1974 has been requested from the City and from County revenue sharing.

For five years the Senior Citizens' Center, Inc. was administered by the Las Animas County Department of Public Welfare (now known as the Department of Social Services), with the assistant director serving as Senior Citizen director on a part-time volunteer basis.

Since 1971 the program has been administered by the Model City Agency with the former coordinator serving as full time director.

ORGANIZATION

The organizational structure of the Center is as follows:

a. nine member board of directors (volunteer)
b. director (paid)
c. assistant to the director (paid)
d. bus-driver — custodian (paid) *
e. member and citizen volunteers for instruction, meals, social activities, fund-raising activities, etc.
f. advisory service from the director of the Department of Social Services and the Model City Project Coordinator (volunteer)

* This position has been a constant problem as the salary for the worker is paid by Operation Mainstream (a manpower training program). The salary is minimal and we find ourselves without this much needed staff member too often for it over burdens our already very busy schedule.

STAFFING

The basic staff of the Trinidad Senior Citizens Center consists of a director, an assistant to the director, and a bus driver-custodian. All policies and activities not defined and outlined in the by-laws originate and are activated by the director with the board's approval. Staff members are under the direct supervision of the project director.

When the occasion and need arises committees are appointed by the board to augment the proposed project, i.e. publicity, meals, parties, fund-raising, etc.

The disposition of available funds comes under the joint control of the board and center director. A basic standard bookkeeping system is utilized as is in most senior citizen centers throughout the nation.

Up to the present time the staffing and administration of the Center has been sufficient, but with program enlargement, whatever additions are needed will be added at the discretion of the board and the director, always with the proviso that funds will be available.

SERVICES BEING OFFERED

Recreational

Because of the nature of the Center, almost any activity lends itself to recreation. However, those activities scheduled primarily as recreational include contract and duplicate bridge, bingo, pool, dominoes, sandbowling, square-dancing, birthday and holiday parties. Bowling and swimming are planned for the near future.

Arts and Crafts

Ceramics, handicrafts, and needlecraft programs (with volunteer professional instruction) offer opportunities for self-expression.

Educational

Drawing from experts in the field, programs have been offered on Medicare, and Medicaid, Frauds and Quacks, Social Security Information, Nutrition and Meal planning, Food purchasing, Care of Fabrics, Food Stamps, Safety, Flower Arranging, etc. At various times we have held classes in Spanish, physical fitness, and are now in the process of organizing a creative writing class.

Meals

Because the need for nutritious meals and for companionship is recognized, a *"mini" lunch* is served every Tuesday. We called it "mini" because we began by serving soup and sandwiches. The response and appreciation for a "nutritious" meal was so great, that we now serve a balanced meal. Seventy-five cents buys a meat dish, vegetable and/or salad, dessert, bread and butter, and a hot drink. We serve seconds to those who are especially hungry and there is a big demand for left-overs for another meal.

Pot-luck lunches are scheduled monthly, followed by slides of Center activities, movies, or other entertainment usually presented by one of the local schools.

All holidays are celebrated with an afternoon tea, featuring appropriate programs and refreshments.

Easter, Thanksgiving, and Christmas dinners are served and taken to shut-ins free of charge. However, donations are accepted to help defray the cost.

One of the favorite activities is the monthly birthday party which honors those who have celebrated a birthday during the month. Each celebrant receives a personally made card, a small gift, and an individual cake. The oldest man and woman receive a special gift and take home a Polaroid snapshot of themselves.

An annual membership dinner is held in January when the entire membership votes for three board members. (Members are elected for three-year terms and cannot succeed themselves for at least one year).

An annual awards banquet is held in May, Senior Citizens month.

Transportaiton

The bus (a 12-passenger van purchased with the last of Title III monies) is available for out-of-town cultural and sight-seeing tours and for transportation to and from the Center for scheduled activities.

Semi-monthly trips to the downtown area for shopping and bill-paying are scheduled to coincide with social security and pension pay days. This service is designed especially for those who have no means of transportation, as Trinidad has no public transit system.

Center personnel or member volunteers regularly do the shopping and bill-paying for those who are handicapped or homebound.

Telephone Reassurance

Telephone calls are regularly made to persons who live alone and home visits are made when it is felt that someone is in need of personal contact and emotional reassurance.

Get-well and sympathy cards are sent and visits made by staff or volunteers.

Newsletter

A monthly newsletter and calendar of events is sent to each member, and to anyone of this age group who is referred to the Center. This provides a means of keeping in touch with persons who do not often come to the Center, but feel that it is part of their world. Special sections of member contributions encourage creative writing and recipe exchanges.

Counseling

Not *per se*, as clinically defined, but a person to person reassurance that someone is interested and cares.

Information and Referral

Health needs, housing, legal aid, doctors, and any emergency situations that arise in the life of a senior citizen are handled by the director and her assistant with the resources and agencies that are at our disposal.

On many occasions the Center is contacted by relatives or friends of senior citizens in this area if the concerned party is unable to locate them. We often go into the home in a functional capacity, i.e. meals, transportation, etc. while a senior citizen is awaiting admission to the hospital or State Nursing Home.

In short we have made every effort to make the Center a one-stop repository of information and referral services.

Center Rental

The Center is available, at a nominal fee, to private individuals who like the home-like atmosphere for their meetings and parties.

It is also available, rent free, to government and service organizations such as Community Action, Model Cities, Girl Scout Leaders, Alcoholics Anonymous, the local Junior College for extension-classes, and others.

At this time I would like to interject some data that, I feel, makes the Trinidad Senior Citizens Center perhaps a little unique in the aged program field.

Trinidad being a community of less than 10,000 people and having a senior citizen population of approximately 2400 is a polyglot of ethnic groups. The basic settlers were the Spanish-American and Anglo-Saxon. In addition to these we have a large scattering of Mediterraneans and Near Easterners. So far, in our activities and concerted efforts at the Center, this heterogeneous environmental element has presented no obstacles — a situation in which I am most pleased. Conversations and contacts with officials and senior citizens from other areas have inclined me to believe that we are most fortunate here not to have ethnic conflicts. Members appreciate and learn cultures and languages from one another.

An annual membership fee of $2.00 is asked, but is not an absolute requirement for membership or participation. The only requirement at the Senior Citizens Center is a minimum age of fifty years. The average age, however, is in the mid seventies.

We have made every effort to involve the low income and minority groups with an appreciable amount of success. However, since I feel very strongly that loneliness is not limited to the poor and/or minority groups only, the Center has membership from all socio-economic levels. Approximately ninety percent are on fixed low incomes, the source of which is social security, old age pension, or a combination of both. Our more "affluent" members are either coal mine or railroad retirees with incomes from both social security and union pensions. Trinidad has few if any residents on the upper economic strata.

The Trinidad Senior Citizens' Center has hopes that in the future all funding would be from one or two sources. This would leave the staff with more time for program and activity planning, and a broader scope of community a tion.

In the immediate future the Center building is to be expanded to almost double the present size. This addition will enable us to serve daily well-balanced meals at the Center and deliver them to homes where they are needed. Trinidad being a depressed area makes this a desirable project for the Center.

We would like to add an on-the-premises small scale health facility, i.e. hearing, visual, and blood-pressure tests.

With the expanded facility we will more firmly implant ourselves into the socio-economic life of the community. Agencies such as legal aid, alcoholics anonymous, mental health, etc. will be given office space for meetings and counseling. We plan to enter into a full scale campaign to increase membership and serve double the twenty percent we now serve.

CHAPTER 10

THE CAPE HENLOPEN
SOCIAL CENTER, INC.

JOSEPH G. ZIEBER

THE need for a Senior Citizens Center in the Rehoboth Beach, Delaware area was recognized in the early 60s, as each church and civic service organization was made aware of the need by their older members. Individual groups were formed but were quite small and did not survive for long. The Protestant Churches then tried rotating a monthly program, but this too was not successful. Late in 1965 all the churches, Catholic and Protestant, in the community banded together and formed a community action group called the Rehoboth United Service Commission (RUSCO). The purpose of the group was to study the numbers and needs of the Senior Citizens to see what was necessary to satisfy these needs.

In late summer 1966 the Soroptomist Club of Eastern Sussex County contacted the Delaware Commission on Aging and requested assistance in the organizing of a Senior Center for Rehoboth Beach. In September a meeting was held by a representative of the Commission on Aging and was attended by representatives of each civic service organization and the members of RUSCO. The Commission representative outlined the procedure required to acquire funds from the Commission if the group could establish the need for a multi-purpose Senior Center and be able to find the necessary local support for matching a grant under the Older Americans Act of 1965 (Title 3).

On November 1, 1966 this group met again and formally organized, electing officers and a board of directors. It was decided to incorporate and the name chosen for the corporation was "The Cape Henlopen Social Center." Purpose: to establish a full-time multi-purpose Senior Citizens Center for the older people of the area known as "the Rehoboth School District." This area included the City of Rehoboth and an area about seven miles to the north, west, and south of the city.

Subsequently, committees developed a constitution and by-laws for the Cape Henlopen Social Center and in December a charter of incorporation was issued by the State of Delaware indicating this was a non-profit, non-sectarian organization to serve the needs of the older people in the area described.

Application was made to the Commission on Aging for a grant under Title 3 of the Older Americans Act. This funding to be 75 percent Federal and 25 percent local. The local funds being either cash or "in-kind."

In December an agreement was reached with the American Legion for the use of their building and equipment, rent free, five days a week, Monday through Friday. The Center to pay all utilities and provide custodial service as required.

This agreement provided the needed local in-kind to support a budget of $12,000 for the first year of operation, the in-kind being $3,000 and the cash funding from the State Commission on Aging being $9,000.

In support of the application for funding the Board of Directors had determined the possible membership to be about 300 from a permanent area population of about 3,000 and had found many older people interested in having a place to meed to improve their social life. The Directors set forth the purposes of the Center to be Social, Recreational and Educational and to provide Counselling, Information, and Referral service as required. The project grant was approved in December 1966 for calendar 1967.

The Board of Directors had been searching and continued to search for a full-time Executive Director for the Center. The salary was set at $5,000 which did not make the job attractive to many qualified people who had family responsibilities. It was not until late February a person was found that was acceptable to the Board and who could accept this salary for a full-time job. The new Executive Director was a retired telephone company executive who had experience in the field of aging through active participation in Telephone Pioneer Life-Member activities and many years of Boy Scout work in the field of crafts and program planning.

Arrangements were made, upon hiring the Executive Director, to open the Center on March 21, 1967. A formal opening and dedication was held on this day. The opening was attended by local and state officials and about 80 senior citizens. No prior registration of Center members had been made. At the end of this opening session 30 people had registered as members of the Center.

A daily schedule of events had been prepared and was presented by the Executive Director. The morning periods from 10 to 12 were used for crafts, e.g., knitting, sewing, leathercraft, basketry, etc., and the afternoons for playing cards or other games. A monthly event was started which has continued with great success all through the years, a birthday party at which volunteers prepare a sandwich lunch (furnished by the Center) and homemade cakes are brought by selected volunteers, to celebrate the birthdays which occur during the month. A point of interest is the publishing of all birthday dates in a monthly news and program letter which is sent to all members— or prospective members — and the sending of a birthday greeting card to each individual on their birthdays. This item seems to be greatly appreciated, indicating personal interest, and also promotes the exchange of personal cards among the members.

We found good acceptance of items which we furnished the local newspapers and radio or TV stations. They gladly publish or announce any items we furnish them, at any time we request. (The material, of course, is neatly prepared and is information about our activities.)

After some experience with various craft items we came to the conclusion that the simple crafts using scrap material and not requiring great skill were the most acceptable.

One of the most frequent requests we get, after instructing in the making or doing of a craft item, is "Would it be all right if I took this home and worked on it tonight? It will help the time to pass." This is particularly true of people who never had a craft or hobby before retirement as many men and women seem to have not had the time to have such things.

On the other hand we found many women who were

accomplished knitters, crocheters, etc., who no longer practiced their craft because there was no family left to do the work for. We encouraged these people to do their thing, some to help others to learn, and later, after accumulating a large number and variety of items, we found we were able to dispose of everything by having a bazaar. Our two bazaars, one in mid-summer and one in December specializing in Christmas decorations and gifts are looked forward to and well patronized by the local citizens.

During the first year the membership slowly grew to about 80, the average daily attendance being about 10. One of the first problems which became apparent was the need of many elderly people for transportation. A small group of volunteers was organized to alleviate their need and since we are mainly a rural area arrangements were made to car pool for those members who still were able to drive an automobile and had a suitable vehicle. The staff, Director and clerks, also provided considerable transportation, particularly special needs such as doctor and hospital visits. This situation is about the same after seven years of operation.

A small amount of money is included in the budget to provide two trips each year to nearby points of interest or entertainment. The cost of transportation is mainly borne by the Center and all other expense is paid by the individual.

During the first year there was a reluctance on the part of the members to confide in and ask for help from the staff. Several meetings were held with speakers from Social Security, Veterans Affairs and other agencies involved in affairs of the elderly. Many surprising things were turned up, such as eligibility for pension or other payment which came as a complete surprise to the individual. Such meetings are a regular part of the program.

Starting in the second year this reluctance disappeared and counselling and information and referral service became, and continues to be, the most important part of our service. There is daily use of these services, there being very few days in a year in which some older person does not seek such help for some problem.

During the second year (1968) the membership grew to about 150 and the daily average attendance to 14.

The budget for the second year was $16,000. The funding was 60%-40%. The Commission on Aging gave us $1,000 of State funds and the local in-kind was made up of free rent, volunteer services to the Center, mainly craft instructions and transportation provided by personal motor vehicles. This matched $10,000 of Title 3 funds.

The third year budget was $16,000. The funding to be 50%-50%. At this time the in-kind rules were changed and it became evident we would need local cash in order to earn the Title 3 funds. Since all local organizations were represented on the Board of Directors each Board member made a personal representation and appeal to his organization. The results were excellent. We have been able to continue all subsequent years on this basis, the local cash given in good-sized sums by the church and civic organizations ranging from $3,000 the third year to $4,500 for the seventh year.

The daily programs are varied from time to time to provide lectures, slide shows, movies, bingo games and card parties. Two craft items have been included for the last 5 years which are very popular, chair caning and oil painting. The Center also has a complete woodworking shop which gets considerable use by the men from time to time as they work on projects for home or make items for sale at the bazaars.

We plan to continue in the same vein, adding new items to the program as they are brought to our attention by the members. The membership in the seventh year is 350 and the daily attendance averages 25.

The Board of Directors and Staff are still seeking a solution to the transportation problem. There is no public transportation anywhere in the area. Two trials have been made of running a scheduled bus service, one using a school bus and one a 10-passenger mini-bus. Our experience indicates the mini-bus to be the most suitable for older people and we are seeking the means of financing such a bus as a part of our program.

The Staff of this Center is an Executive Director and two part-time clerk-assistants who split the complete week between them. Volunteer help is used for some of the craft instruction and members of the Board are available for counselling and information and referral if required.

The greatest thing we dispense is sociability. Over the years we have seen many friendships made and life becoming more pleasant and secure. This is a growing retirement area, many older people finding mobile homes suitable for their financial situation. The Center becomes a focal point in their lives, taking the place of their former activities connected with their working lives. The members are mainly middle-class Americans. All religions are represented but no Spanish-Americans or Blacks use the Center although many Blacks have used our information and referral service.

We are very proud of an often heard comment made by people visiting the Center for the first time and by some who have been members for years,

"My, this is a comfortable place, I really feel at home here."

CHAPTER 11

THE PROGRAM OF
SENIOR CITIZENS SERVICE, INC.,
CLEARWATER, FLORIDA

ELMER H. SHAFER

A PROGRAM OF ACTION
PURPOSES SPECIFIED IN CHARTER
COMMUNITY CHARACTERISTICS
EVIDENCE OF COMMUNITY INTEREST AND PARTICIPATION
OBJECTIVES
ADULT EDUCATION
EMPLOYMENT
HEALTH AND HEALTH SERVICES
HOBBIES AND CRAFTS
HOUSING
LEGAL AID
RECREATION AND SOCIAL ACTIVITIES
RETIREE VISITATION
SECOND CAREERS
HAVEN HOUSE
OPERATIONS OF SCS
FUNDING

THIS section will deal with the program of one of the older non-profit, private organizations in the country, providing multi-services to the elderly. It will cover the founding, objectives, program, methods of operation, growth and scope of the corporation. Ormond E. Loomis, primary founder, was president from the beginning until he died in the fall of 1971 at the age of 84. He was so sincere in his efforts to help others, he found ready cooperation from many who donated both time and money to what they were sure would become a very successful operation.

Early in November, 1958, a series of weekly conferences was begun with representatives of the leading service clubs, churches, philanthropic and civic organizations in Upper Pinellas County. Out of these conferences, and the facts obtained, it became evident that a large and growing need existed for aid to the elderly, not only among those of low, inadequate incomes, but also among those of ample means who were unoccupied and felt lonely, detached and unprepared for retirement.

Conferences of the participating groups culminated in the decision to form a non-profit clearing-house organization designed to deal with the obvious and most important facets of need. Scrupulous effort was made to design an organization and program which would invite the participation of existing organizations and local procedures so that no new activities would duplicate or encroach upon the programs of existing organizations.

A service exchange corporation was created as a cooperative ally to supplement rather than replace or impair the services of other organizations. Formal organization began January 24, 1959, when the Service Exchange was chartered as a non-profit, non-sectarian corporation. A year later it was reincorporated under Florida law with its present title, Senior Citizens Services, Inc.

By provision of the U.S. Bureau of Internal Revenue, it is registered as a tax exempt institution. It is a business operated by business standards, corporation-designed, to deal with the realities of those, whether handicapped or otherwise, who desire to live out their years in dignity, comfort, and enjoyment as respected and useful members of society.

A PROGRAM OF ACTION

Built on the thesis that life is valuable and ought to be useful the corporation has made progress in implementing its belief that most people are normal in their desire both to give and receive, regardless of age or economic status. Giving and receiving can never be measured wholly in terms of money. Often they are measured without price or possibility of monetary rating. Instead they can be interpreted only in satisfaction, dignity, and temperate pride. For each, the crux of the problem of adjustment to older age is a personal decision as to what to do with time and other resources. There is a statistical evidence that sudden, complete idleness in retirement, after an active career, is a short route to the grave. In the opinion of a growing number of senior citizens no person of sound health and faculties has any right, at whatever age, to live for or unto himself alone. Still, with a few — particularly among those who have a well-filled purse — the image and rewards of usefulness are not clear.

It is the opinion of the officers and directors of Senior Citizens Service Corporation that the problem is not exclusively the aged individual but of the community as well. By community leadership and services, the life of the individual and the community can be greatly enriched.

PURPOSES SPECIFIED IN CHARTER

As stated in Article 11 of its Charter, the corporation "shall be exclusively charitable towards giving help and guidance to elderly citizens." In furtherance of these purposes the corporation undertakes, among other things, to:

(a) Provide a clearing house or exchange for the purpose of seeking, assembling, and making use of human and material organizations, corporations, service clubs, churches, fraternal, patriotic, civic, business, benevolent organizations interested in the welfare and problems of elderly persons;

(b) Deal with the physical, medical, legal, educational, economic, housing, and retirement problems, as well as the social, recreational and creative needs of elderly persons according to highest ethics and standards; and

(c) Organize, supervise, direct, and participate with others in the organization, supervision, and direction of mutually helpful projects and community facilities for vocational, educational, avocational, and recreational needs and activities of elderly persons.

Twenty-one Leaders of the Greater Clearwater community constitute the Board of Directors of the corporation. An Advisory Board consists of fifteen members, hold three meetings year, called by the president for specific help in advancing the work of the corporation. They represent the business, financial, civic, professional, and social organizations of the area.

The organization had no pattern or precedent known to its leaders, except that provided by business corporations in which directors are chosen to represent membership and experience in other organizations. Acknowledging that backgrounds of diversified experience and interests have a value in corporate activities, the membership ofhhe S.C.S. Board of Directors is made up of leaders with various backgrounds and affiliations.

COMMUNITY CHARACTERISTICS

Clearwater and Upper Pinellas areas served by SCS, has a population of approximately 240,000 people. One third of these people are retirees. Since this county was regarded as the most reasonable area in which to retire, large numbers of retired persons came to Pinellas starting early in the fifties. Many of these are now in the "over 75" group and many have been left alone.

Perhaps, because the vast majority in our area of Florida's West Coast have retired with some life savings, the income level is higher than in non-retirement communities, but the pattern still provides the three general categories, — rich, poor, and moderates, with a few who move across borders by the pressures of favorable or adverse circumstances. In these last few years, we have seen inflation in general and the extreme high cost of medical and other professional services cut deeply into the value of their savings and fixed income.

Although their interests and needs vary and differ, they have common characteristics — their desire for compansionship and general acceptance, their search for attractive, diverting recreation, their need of church life and spiritual supports, their desire for good health, purposeful interests, and security. In these respects, they conform to the common pattern.

To serve the needs of its residents, the general Clearwater community has the normal number of civic, social, religious, and welfare agencies. Churches, Chamber of Commerce, trade and civic organizations, recreation, art, craft, hobby and fraternal clubs do well in holding their members and inviting the participation of newcomers. But often, both among established residents and the new, there is need (particularly among the elderly) of accurate information about the agencies and resources available for their benefit.

EVIDENCE OF COMMUNITY INTEREST AND PARTICIPATION

From its beginning the Corporation has enjoyed remarkable cooperation and support from local citizens and organizations. At first it was given rent free office space on the second floor of a small office building. Later the Mayor and City Council of Clearwater provided larger, rent-free quarters on the first floor of a city-owned building adjoining its Public Library, centrally located and near parking lots. The larger quarters, including utilities, provided without cost, give substantial evidence of local interest, confidence and backing. Subsequently when the City decided to tear down the building and construct an addition to the Public Library, it gave the Corporation another centrally located office building half of which was occupied by its Civil Service officers.

Within two years the Corporation had outgrown this alloted space and the City gave the free use of a centrally located eight room office building with a large adjoining parking lot. It is here that the organization has its business headquarters today.

OBJECTIVES

As a 100% volunteer organization, the work of SCS was accomplished by forming committees. Each committee chairman was chosen for his desire to provide a service to deal with a certain needs area. He then went about the task of finding suitable people to serve on the committee who would have special knowledge and interest necessary to design and implement the service. Nine such committees were formed. These committees concentrate on:

    1. Adult Education
    2. Employment
    3. Health and Health Service
    4. Hobbies and Crafts
    5. Housing
    6. Legal Aid
    7. Recreational and Social Activity
    8. Retirement and Visitation
    9. Second Careers

The chairmen and members of the Operating Committees, in cooperation with the Executive Director and the officers, work together to carry out their distinctive services. In no case is their activity intended to replace or encrouch upon the work of existing agencies. Rather, wherever appropriate organizations and services exist for senior citizens, they seek to supplement instead of in any way supplant the efforts of other organizations.

Upper Pinellas County is fortunate to have among its residents a large number of executives who have retired from business corporations of national prominence who are disposed to give of their time and talents to public service. The list also includes professional men and women of distinguished careers in colleges, universities, and public life. On them our officers and committees draw for special services as needs arise.

An indication of the functions and objectives of each of the nine operating committees follows:

ADULT EDUCATION

Aware that education is opportunity and that many senior citizens are retiring physically before they are ready, if ever, to retire mentally, the committee on Adult Education and Counseling took steps to assure them every possible means of developing their latent talents, — either for personal profit, public service, or intellectual satisfaction.

Particularly concerned with the leisure time development of talents and abilities in the arts, crafts, technical skills, and cultural pursuits, the committee found the Adult Educational

Department of the Pinellas County School System ready and
willing to cooperate in finding proper teachers and developing
courses for many unusual subjects requested by those of mature
years, each at nominal cost. The subjects range from finger
painting to astronomy. However, we are now offering in our
facilities more helpful courses, such as Lip Reading, Braille, Care
of Convalescents and Home, Law for Laymen, Avoidance of
Fraud, Nutrition, and Planned Spending. Many other courses are
available at various locations and schools designed for the retiree.

Not infrequently a retired educator or artisan, with a lifetime of
experience, offer his or her services gratis for the benefit of oldsters
agreeing, perhaps, with Diogenes, "Education is the best
viaticum of old age."

EMPLOYMENT

Many senior citizens have retired without adequate incomes.
Others undertake to live with incomes below a normal
subsistence level. Only through full or part-time employment can
they maintain their place as independent, self-respecting
members of society. Many who have incomes of less than half
their preretirement level are forced to adjust to a lower standard of
living. They manage to keep a semblance of comfort and well-
being until sickness or emergency develops when they move from
the fringe of financial competence of indigency.

The Committee on Employment seeks to discover job
opportunities for qualified senior citizens who either, because of
pressing need or enforced idleness, seek regular or part-time
employment. Experience of the Committee over the past 10 years
indicates that, increasingly, employers are recognizing values in
the services of older workers not common among younger
workers. Their experience, knowledge, interest and attitudes are
generally superior. They are less likely to be clock-watchers, less
often diverted by outside engagements, and less inclined to find
excuses for slipshod efforts. In fact, some of our senior citizens are
being employed as examples of industry and efficiency, very
much as the farmer (a generation ago) used a steady, reliable
work-horse as a team mate for a sprightly young horse in

training.

Job offerings vary by seasons and economic conditions, but the number and variety available to seniors have increased with the Committe's concentration on their employment. Functioning through its professional staff, the Committee seeks to connect job-seekers with prospective employers. Currently an average of 150 placements are made each month, 60 percent men and 40 percent women.

HEALTH AND HEALTH SERVICES

Health is an elemental need of life. To be healthy contributes to physical mental, social and spiritual vitality. Maintenance of health and vigor increases in difficulty with age. Disorders which develop or become chronic with advancing years become more troublesome and costly.

Health, as a major concern of older people is the special concern of our Committee on Health and Health Services. The Committee recognizes and accepts the conclusion of practicing physicians and public health officers expressed in the state and national conferences that "the promotion of optimal health is a community as well as an individual responsibility, and that health is a function of the community's total way of life, and planning for Health should be correlated with planning for economic and social well-being." In its local area of activity the Committee on Health and Health Services is made up of a representative group of leading physicians, nursing home administrators and public health officials.

Probably no question is being more widely debated throughout the UNITED States than the cost of medicine, medical and hospital services. Its prominence in the lives of senior citizens and its urgence among those of low income make it a major concern for our community. Because of this situation the Committee is deeply involved in dealing with the problems of institutions, as well as of individuals.

The Health Committee with the cooperation of the Pinellas County Health Department has established Glaucoma and Diabetes screenings at our Haven House Community Center.

These are free of charge to those who make scheduled appointments in advance in regular weekly sessions.

The Health Committee has succeeded in interesting the State of Florida and the Florida Blue Cross in establishing a Home Health Care program in Pinellas County as a pilot project for the State. It will be the means that will allow doctors to release patients from the hospitals sooner than they normally would thereby reducing their cost of care as well as to free hospital beds. The program will follow the best experience of over 100 such programs now operating in other states. After experience in Pinellas County The Home Health Care plan would be extended to other Urban areas of the State.

This Committee has also built a large inventory of wheel chairs, walkers, canes, crutches, equipment for the sick room and many types of convalescent aids, which are loaned free to anybody having a need for as long as the need exists. These items have been donated by those who no longer have a need for a particular item, knowing that many older Americans depend on SCS for such equipment when the need arises.

HOBBIES AND CRAFTS

Many retirees were found to be interested in arts and crafts. Some were actually experts and became volunteers, teaching arts as well as various crafts. This work is being done today at our Haven House, a Community Center, which will be explained later in this chapter.

The great need, however, was an outlet for the articles as produced. So, in 1964 the Senior Citizens Craft Center Gift Shop was founded. The Pinellas County Board of Public Instruction gave us long-term use of the physical education building of an old Junior High School Complex. This masonry building, in good condition, was renovated by several volunteers, and is now our Craft Center. Two large rooms serve as display area while others are used for offices and surplus inventory. All articles submitted for sale are examined by a committee of judges who pass upon quality, price and estimated sales potential. The Center is open daily, except Sunday, from 10 AM to 4:30 PM, and manned by unpaid volunteers who sell the products of more than 400 consignors. This property was recently purchased by SCS, while balance of school property will be developed into High Rise Apartments by private purchaser.

All products displayed and sold at the Craft Gift Center are handmade locally by senior citizens of Upper Pinellas County. Nothing is purchased from outside or for resale. The variety of products offered and the standard of values have gained approval and increasing patronage. In 1972 the gross sales amounted to $63,000 and the consignors received 80 percent of this. The whole operation is now self sustaining on 20 percent of sales.

HOUSING

The Committee on Housing was created to provide more adequate housing for low income senior citizens. After surveying the needs and income levels of those in the area, with the advice of the area office of Federal Housing Administration, the first project was developed on a 36 acre attractive water front property on the bayside of Clearwater. The design of the project included 310 garden apartments of efficienty, 1 BR and 1 Bt variety. In addition to the garden apartments, an eight story building provided 96 club type rooms with food service on the ground floor. This was a joint venture with the United Church of Christ. It was opened in April '65 and has become a substantial asset to the people of Clearwater.

The second and most recent activity of the Housing Committee was the promotion of Prospect Towers. Starting as a 202 program under HUD, it was later financed through the FHA 236 restructured program. Costing three and one-half million dollars, standing 17 stories, and providing housing for over 300 retirees, in 96 efficiencies and 112 one-bedroom apartments. First tenants moved in December 30th, 1971 and it was fully occupied by June 1st 1972. There is a waiting list for these apartments at the present time. Rent structure is $80 per month for efficiencies and $107 per month for one-bedrooms, with all utilities paid, including all heat and air-conditioning.

This committee now has their sights set on providing new

housing of "congregate living" facilities. Housing of the room and board type, with limited health services, is very much in demand and very little to be offered in Florida at the present time, within the means of those who need it most.

LEGAL AID

The original committee on Legal Aid, was made up of some attorneys, as well as business men of the community. They were charged with urging the Bar Association to develop cooperation through their Legal Aid Society with Senior Citizens Services Inc.

It was found that many retirees became involved in cases of fraud, swindle, extortion, deception, as well as warranty and landlord problems. Some needed legal services, while other cases were misunderstandings. Counseling at SCS headquarters, with a little help, satisfied most cases and some indigents were referred to the Legal Aid Society. Others were given the choice of several attorneys in their area, practicing in the type of services with which they needed help.

Legal Aid, like other professional services, is difficult to provide to those who are not really indigent but who can afford very little such expense. The Bar Association throughout the country, have been trying to improve their relations with the public in this area.

RECREATION AND SOCIAL ACTIVITIES

The Committee on Recreation is charged with the responsibility of making full use of existing recreational facilities of our community available to retired men and women at low or moderate cost. The Committee endeavors to stimulate interest among elderly citizens in learning how to play and to keep physically and mentally fit and enjoyably active. To achieve this objective it seeks to provide information to elderly residents and newcomers about types and sources of recreational resources which are locally available.

Florida's Gulf Coast communities offer many attractive, well-known recreational facilities — both indoor and outdoor. These

194   *Service Programs for the Older American*

include fishing and boating, bowling and shuffling, gardening and golfing, beachcombing and photography, bird and other nature studies.

The Committee undertakes to make useful information available to newcomers and those in search of attractive diversions. Its services supplement those provided by City Recreation Departments and Hobby Clubs, and by community organizations in their occasional or specialized programs.

Each Holiday Season, on the Saturday before Christmas, a large variety show is staged in the Clearwater Municipal Auditorium, in cooperation with the City Parks and Recreation Department, as well as the Local Musicians Union. Business men provide as many as 30 door prizes, (mostly dinners for two at the better restaurants) and entertainers in the area donate their services. It is a gala affair and all free to retirees.

Again in May, (Senior Citizens Month) a similar show and dance is provided for retirees at no charge. The high-light of this affair, is usually a prominent speaker from Washington talking about Social Security benefits, aging programs, etc.

The Committee also developed a Travel Section. It is one of our busiest departments today. Last year we used 98 charter buses and carried over 6,000 (with some duplications) to various attractions from Key West to the Smokey Mountains of North Carolina. New Orleans was also a very popular trip. Many older retirees are afraid to drive on the busy roads for any distance. Others are alone and may not even have a car. It is a much needed service to these people, and they love being with those of their own age and going places with all the details taken care of and the tour under the direction of trained conductors. Our charges are as low as we can make them for the contributing members of the organization. However, those who are not members pay a little higher price. This is to encourage those who want the service to become members. It is a non-profit operation because the excess over cost, just about pays the overhead for the department's percentage of the SCS headquarters overall operation cost. Because of such activities, we built a membership of over 4,000 people, growing each month.

RETIREE VISITATION

The initial function of the Committee on Retirement Benefits was limited to assistance to retirees in obtaining income, for which they qualified, from pensions, welfare, insurance annuities, bequests, Social Security and other sources.

The organization and development of a visiting and companion service grew out of an expanding need. It has become a two-way program which benefits both the generous giver and the dependent receiver. A large committee was needed to handle the many requests for help. The committee itself acted as leaders and would assign the various calls to one of their volunteers living in the area from which the call emanated. A typical call is the emergency transportation call. Somebody must get to a certain doctor or hospital for a treatment at a certain time, but has nobody, or any transportation, and can't really afford the cost of waiting taxis. Other calls for help, usually for a person living alone, run from A to Z. Sometimes the Welfare department is called in to take over cases found by this committee. In 1972, over 1,000 hours of volunteer service and nearly 5,000 miles of driving resulted in helping 828 people. Also during the year 28 people volunteered to visit shut-ins, and 400 such visits were made.

SECOND CAREERS

The Committee on Second Careers is the ninth of our Operating Committees. It was created to discover and make use of latent interests and talents of retired men and women of unusual experience and success. It is well known that many in their retirement or bonus years are still unsatisfied by their achievements. Some desire to renew cherished purposes which in the preoccupations of an active business or professional life have been set aside or undeveloped.

On the negative side, the Committee is aware that retirement, whether forced or voluntary, can be injurious to health and human relations if it results in idleness, or self-indulgence. On the positive side, the Committee recognizes that added years provided by the increasing span of life, if given in service to others can extend the years of mental, social, and spiritual growth.

The committee as first organized, consisted of retired Bankers, Business Executives, Manufacturers, Public Service Officials, and other such members. Their efforts were directed chiefly to various types of public service especially those of local concern, and to interest all retirees in a second career by actively participating in community activities.

In their search for service that would compliment our objectives, "Insurance Service" was made available to retirees in the area. A deputy Insurance Commissioner from the Florida State Insurance Commissioner's office spends whatever time is necessary to see 10 to 15 people one day each week. They take care of unpaid claims, cancellations of policies, and many other problems a person may have with insurance companies. Over 600 retirees received this service in 1972.

HAVEN HOUSE

This Community Center is a large house that was formerly the Presbyterian Manse in Clearwater. A beautiful home overlooking Clearwater Bay, became available in 1968 for about the value of the land. SCS purchased the property for use as a Center with funds from the sale of some Eckerd stock given to the corporation in 1965 by Jack Eckerd, founder of Jack Eckerd Corp. It is open free of charge to all older Americans and the calendar of activities fills the entire week, except Saturday. Craft workshops and games are provided along with Health Screenings and various types of entertainment. Sunday programs, usually with overflowing attendance, consist of Travelogs, Recitals, and Sing-a-longs. At the present time, the City of Clearwater is planning a roadway that will run directly through this property and Haven House will be rebuilt by SCS on another downtown property that will eventually be the site of the SCS headquarters as well as the Craft Center Gift Shop. When Haven House is rebuilt, it will be doubled in square footage and will include a Day Care Center for the elderly. The auditorium will be suitable for seating 200 people. This is a 100 percent volunteer operation, with only two hostesses, being paid on the same basis as those employees of SCS.

OPERATIONS OF SCS

At the present time, the office of SCS is staffed with six people who receive approximately $1.60 per hour for four days' work from 9 AM to 4 PM, with the noon hour off for lunch. The office is open Monday through Friday. Lunch is usually prepared by some of the volunteers and/or staff, who have brought a few things in for the refrigerator. Other items necessary such as coffee and a few staples are purchased by the organization from the petty cash fund. Because there are few who leave for the lunch hour, the office remains open and service goes on.

A tight ship is evidenced by the over-all operating cost in 1972 of only $36,000 including the greater part of the salary of the Executive Director. All other work is handled by volunteers working with the staff people. The executive director received a small part of his overall salary from Prospect Towers, of which he is administrator. He also directs the affairs of the Craft Center and the Haven House operations.

FUNDING

As stated in the beginning, Senior Citizens Services Inc., began as a 100 percent volunteer operation, with no paid employees of any kind. During the early sixties, Ormond Loomis, president and founder, staffed the employment department and one or two clerks on a part-time basis at a minimum hourly rate. Funds were obtained from outstanding citizens and businesses of the community.

Beginning with the fiscal year of 1967 (July 1, 1966) after the passage of the Older Americans Act of 1965, SCS became the first such agency in the State of Florida to be funded under Title III of the ACT. The funding was made available for the purpose of further expansion of the services, through the use of volunteers. At this point, an executive director was employed and the staff was increased to six. Senior Citizens Services participated in the Title III program on the basis of 75 percent of budget for 1967, 60 percent during fiscal year of 1968 and 50 percent for 1969. In 1969 amendments to the Act permitted further funding by the state and SCS participated on a 50 percent basis during the calendar year of 1970.

Since 1970 we have continually increased our membership and activities, with the Recreation and Tour Department, providing their own cost (over 50% of $36,000 budget) making the organization self subsistent.

Funding such an organization in many areas of the country, as well as in the state of Florida, we have seen various types of senior centers started. Often they were Information and Referral operations, with plans to add services as they progressed. The organization was composed of a Board of Directors and a fully paid staff, headed by a project director. Too often this required a fairly high budget, making the 25 percent matching funds for the first year of a Title III program hard to put together. Even when it was accomplished few were able to say where the 40 percent matching funds for the second year would come from.

In many such organizations, the founders were not always sincere in their efforts, nor sufficiently aware of what they were trying to accomplish. Because of the funding was available, they thought all they had to do was hire somebody who was supposed to know how to run the center and apply for the funds. The results have been extremely disastrous in a great number of cases.

In planning such a service for older Americans, real and sincere leaders of the community must be involved. They must understand exactly why such an organization is needed and what they hope to accomplish. They must have sufficient interest to contribute to the cause and to persuade their friends and city fathers to do likewise. If they organize under a good charter and with definite goals, and business principles, good people will become involved. Soon, they will find they do have good community acceptance and they are well on their way. It is imperative to keep the first year budget low, so that the second year can be expanded to bring about a greater cash flow. As the organization progresses, "in-kind" matching funds will be easier to obtain.

Again, we say it is necessary to use all available services in the community to help in the overall services being provided to the seniors. As an example, classes operated by the Adult Education division of the Public School System can be credited to the organization as "in-kind matching funds" to the extent of the actual dollars paid the teachers for those classes taught at the senior center. Any such contribution of the Health Department of the County would likewise count.

Good planning and the use of all available help with good business sense, is a must, however, the use and retention of volunteers is also important to a successful operation. Volunteers must be placed in a position where their time and talents are properly recognized and used to the best advantage. This does not mean that a retired physician must serve in health service only. He has a great deal to offer and has been dealing with people in the most intimate way all his life. He can handle any number of areas of help, and will, if the jobs assigned dignify his experience and position in life. New volunteers must be counseled and placed properly if you intend to receive the value of their highest and best use, or even retain them for any period of time. And, as time goes on, they need attention and need to be consulted with so that they know they are needed and are providing a service.

If a person wished to start a fine restaurant, he would certainly find out what is needed to operate such a place. He would do some research and visit other places with the kind of reputation and food he wanted. But, too often, those involved with programs such as we have in mind, become involved in name only. It is up to the persons starting the organization to see that all who intend to serve are completely aware of the need and the ways the organization intends to meet the needs.

Since the White House Conference of 1971, new programs have been designed. Some will receive funding and others will be scrapped. There is still a need to design programs that will do more than fill one need. If we can provide good, well planned congregate living for those in the upper increments of aging, we will with one program cover Housing, Health, Nutrition, and to the most extent, Transportation.

CHAPTER 12

SERVICES FOR THE OLDER AMERICAN IN THE SHENANDOAH VALLEY OF VIRGINIA

DORIS ANNE MILLER

THE Valley Program for Aging Service, Inc. is in the Sixth Planning District of Virginia which covers the Central Shenandoah Valley. This geographic area, located in the Western part of the state in the heart of the Shenandoah Valley, is primarily a rural area. It is bordered on the Alleghany Mountains on the west and the Blue Ridge Mountains on the east.

The Central Shenandoah Planning District has a population of 186,306 and has a land area of 3,439 square miles, making it the largest planning district in the state of Virginia. Although the principal occupation is agriculture, the valley is fast becoming urbanized and is dotted with large and numerous industrial operations that cover a wide variety of industrial products. Due to the fact that the district has mountainous areas that are a part of the National Park and Wildlife Management Land, recreation is also becoming a major source of income.

According to the 1970 census data, 31% of those aged 60 and over residing in the Central Shenandoah Valley are at or below the poverty level for the area. Persons 60 years of age and older represent 14.1% of our total population. This translates into 26,293 persons. These figures do not include institutionalized persons who are being returned to the communities in this area. Western State Mental Hospital, a large state supported mental institution is located in the city of Staunton and has a geriatric

C.S.P.D.C. Comprehensive Plan for Area Wide Model Program for Aged, prepared by Glen Campbell — Senior Planner.

census of approximately 3,000 individuals. The hospital is under mandate to reduce this census by 10% each year. A pre-screening program has been initiated by the institution to reduce the number of geriatric admissions to the hospital. Therefore, as one can see with this number of geriatric patients re-entering the local communities and with the pre-screening program being instituted there is a substantial need for a comprehensive service program for the older American in the Central Shenandoah Valley area.

Some of the collateral facilities which are available to provide various services to the older American in the Central Shenandoah Valley include the 19 nursing homes which are now operational and have a total bed capacity of 683. There are also a limited number of homes for the older american providing residential services but not nursing services. There are foster care homes available within the valley area; however, the exact number are not available at this time. Another prime service agency for the older american located in this area is the District Home. The District Home is a residential nursing care facility for the indigent older american from Augusta County and surrounding counties.

There are four active chapters of the American Association of Retired Persons with a total membership of approximately 1200 persons. Other Senior citizens clubs and organizations are affiliated with various recreation departments in the area and with churches. The majority of the members of these organizations are middle to upper income level individuals who are also physically and mentally able retirees. However, there is a tremendous gap in services for those of middle to lower income levels and for those who are less capable physically and mentally. The aging program in the Central Shenandoah Valley was established to assist in filling this gap in services.

In November, 1970, the Board of Directors of the Valley Workshops, Inc., secured a five month Planning and Development Grant from the Administration on Aging in H.E.W. Region III through the Division of State Planning and Community Affairs, Office on Aging. The purpose of this planning grant was to determine the needs of the elderly in the catchment area which included the county of Augusta and the adjoining cities of Waynesboro and Staunton. This catchment area represents a limited part of the Central Shenandoah Valley. However, it is most centrally located in the Sixth Planning District. The reason for the geographic limitations on the planning grant was to gain some initial experience relative to the needs for service programs and to develop some predictable measure of the commitment of funding which would be required for a comprehensive service programming.

The Valley Workshop, the sponsoring organization for the aging program, is a private non-profit corporation with traditional sheltered workshops in four locations serving the vocationally handicapped. The clients of the Valley Workshops are for the most part young adults referred from the local counselors of the Department of Vocational Rehabilitation. The emphasis in the Valley Workshops Program is on evaluation and work adjustment training with the ultimate goal being the vocational placement of the individual in the community in competitive employment.

Members of the Board and professional staff of the Valley Workshops, Inc. were interested in determining the needs of the aging population in the communities. Until this time there had been no organized effort at any such survey nor had any planning activities been undertaken. The initial efforts undertaken at this time included personal interviews, planning sessions and talks with social services departments, health and recreation departments, ministerial associations, senior club groups, civic and community organizations. These meetings were carried on with the expressed purpose of determining the existing services being offered to the aging population, the determination of existing needs and the climate within the communities relative to the needs of the aging and the location of aging services in the hierarchy of the communities.

During this period, plans were underway for the 1970 White House Conference on Aging. Because of the interest being shown in the Shenandoah Valley, a steering committee for a district-wide conference was appointed. Representatives from agencies, organizations, churches, and retired persons were assigned to planning committees. The first pre-White House Conference on a district-wide level for Virginia was held in Waynesboro, Virginia in February 1971. Over 200 persons were registered for this day long conference which included workshops sessions. Workshop leaders for these workshop sessions in the conference consisted of professionals and interested individuals from the local health department, the various social service agencies, the Mental Health Association and the local chapters of the American Association of Retired Persons. In order to better view the problems in serving the older american, a special workshop was set up for area professionals to deal with local aging problems and develop possible solutions for these problems. Fifteen agencies and organizations participated in this conference and the various workshop sessions.

The suggestions arising from this conference included:

1. Workshops and Planning Sessions for Professionals and Semi-Professionals should be developed. The basic purpose of these sessions would be for information sharing among various agencies both city, county and state in order to cut through as much of the bureaucratic red tape as possible to improve services to older Americans.
2. Aftercare services need to be improved substantially. Some people are working through official aftercare agencies to help furnish transportation and offer friendly gestures to older Americans. Presently, these people are working through local churches. Case histories disclose much help is being rendered from these efforts. But many more people and more organizational strength are needed to expand this effort. Official aftercare agencies and private agencies are hampered by a lack of community support. Therefore, efforts should be mobilized to increase awareness and community support.
3. Volunteer agencies have dire needs for volunteer support groups working in the community and residential care institutions. There is a substantial need for more volunteers and a need for better trained volunteers. The agencies require better and more organized training to improve the skills of volunteers in the volunteer work which they do.
4. There is a gap in communication between institutions discharging older Americans and the social services agencies

within the communities to which these older Americans are discharged. This communication gap is severe and has considerable impact on the quality of life of the older American. Work should be done to improve the level of communication between various institutions which are sending older Americans back to local communities.

5. The various news media, press, radio and television must assume a larger share of the responsibility for developing community awareness. This can be done through news coverage of various conferences, meetings, service programs and needs of older Americans. The news media should help produce programs for the older American dealing with the older American in an effort not only to inform the older American but also to modify the public attitudes about the problems of aging. Critically needed are informational programs geared to the older American with limited income and limited education.

6. A considerable need of the older American is for income supplementation or the opportunity to become workers in an area of work which is compatible with their physical and mental condition. In order to provide this service transportation and various vocational equipment is essential. Therefore, money in the form of grants and contributions need to be solicited in order to provide the mechanism for people over 65 to become employed either on a temporary part-time or full-time basis.

7. Not only is it important to identify the services needed for the older American it is imperative that the size, extent, desires and motivational level of the aging population must ba assessed. Therefore, a survey must be developed and initiated to answer these questions prior to the initiation of aging services.

8. A central agency needs to be established in order to coordinate, correlate and initiate aging services within the geographical area. This agency would also provide information referral and tracking services for the older American in order to inform him as to what services are available, where they are available and the criteria of eligibility for those services.

As a result of the interest which was ascertained as a result of the planning grant direct services for the older American were initiated prior to the expiration of the planning and development grant. The Waynesboro East Augusta Mental Health Association contributed their local United Giver's Fund monies to move their Day Center for aftercare persons under the Aging Program of the Valley Workshops, Inc. By using a workshop bus, transportation was provided to those persons involved in the aftercare program. Sub-contract work from industry provided to the workshops was furnished the Day Center clients for a work-therapy program. Contrary to some opinions, we found that money is a prime motivating factor for the handicapped and/or the aging as well as the general population. Also during the planning period, other work-therapy programs were developed at the District Home and at the DeJarnette State Hospital. All three of these work-therapy programs were part-time. The DeJarnette program was operated three afternoons per week, the District Home program was operated three mornings per week and the Day Care Center was operated two days per week.

As a result of available resources, community needs and community requests by April 1971 concrete program components had emerged in a priority fashion. The required funding for the local match of the Administration on Aging, Title III grant application was approved by the governing bodies of Waynesboro, Virginia, Staunton, Virginia and Augusta County.

The three major components were (and continue to be):
1. Income Supplementation
2. Transportation
3. Information and Referral

Basic objectives of the program through the establishment of Senior Centers include:
1. To provide the following direct services — transportation, income supplementation, information and referral to the low income, isolated, and/or homebound older american.
2. To assist older persons in remaining in their homes through community support by providing beneficial programs and social outlets.
3. To integrate persons from retirement homes, aftercare facilities and others into aging center programs.
4. To provide the middle income, talented, retired

individual with meaningful activity and volunteer roles.

5. To help with in-service training for college students studying in the area of gerontology.

During 1971, the existing programs were expanded, the Waynesboro Senior Service Center and the Staunton Senior Service Center were opened.

Public transportation in the planning district is non-existant except for a transit system in the city of Staunton. Most small communities within the rural area did not have taxi service. Therefore, through the use of the workshop buses, the transportation project was able to begin. The mini-bus was used on a regular basis to transport persons to center programs. Volunteers were transporting individuals to various physician's offices and other medical services. This was an extremely limited activity, however, the Waynesboro Junior Woman's Club enlisted the help of the Jaycees and the community in a trading stamp drive to purchase an "Aging Bus." Eventually enough stamps were collected to redeem as the required cash necessary for the matching share of a grant written for the purpose of purchasing a bus. In May, 1972, the new Aging Bus made its first run.

By mid 73, the Board of Directors of the Valley Workshops, Inc., realized the aging program had grown to the extent it no longer needed the support of the Valley Workshops, Inc. and should be encouraged to develop as a separate private non-profit board. This very positive move by the Valley Workshops, Inc. has resulted in the development of the Valley Program for Aging Services, Inc. and the extension of services to other areas of the Central Shenandoah Valley.

The planning in each community involved local agencies, both public and private along with the retired population. The center locations were secured by residents of the community and all (seven) centers currently operate in rent free facilities such as churches, vacant schools, municipal buildings, city-owned buildings, nursing homes and a privately owned hotel. The community expressed an interest, genuine concern and their willingness to assist in the planning, operation and use of local funds and volunteers before the centers opened.

The retired person is much more than a member of the retired community. He or she is a retired something be it teacher, minister, engineer, plumber, painter, banker, attorney, doctor, secretary, social worker or other. Many willingly contribute their skills and knowledge in total center operation as invaluable volunteers and/or part-time staff to keep up to date on their skills. As many have said, "I now have a reason to get up in the mornings." These individuals are personally rewarded by new associations and the realization that their contribution is vitally needed in the life and growth of their center. As persons grow older, less mobile and more removed from close associations with family members and friends it is increasingly important for them to cultivate new friends and broaden their hobbies and interests. The center is a good nucleous for active participation and leaves little time for depression and anxiousness. Regular clients develop relationships not unlike a family unit.

Over a three year period, persons involved in the income supplementation project of the Aging Program have earned over $80,000. Presently there are about 75 persons per week taking advantage of this program. The elderly in many different settings have been involved in this income supplementation program. Settings such as a home for the aged indigent, the geriatric wards of two mental hospitals, the individuals who are homebound as well as regular senior citizen service center clients. Some persons worked only a week or two, a few have participated since the beginning of the program, but an overwhelming majority are interested in this facet of the comprehensive service program. Sub-contract work such as that secured in sheltered workshops from local industry, which is figured on a piece-rate basis and is usually transported is ideal for this type of program. All work is subjected to time motion studies to enable an average worker to earn at least a minimum wage. However, because the majority of aging individuals have other handicaps such as stroke, blindness, emotional problems, severe limitations on mobility, etc. few are able to reach this production level. The sociability of being with others, having something to do and feeling the responsibility of getting the work out makes the program truly a work-therapy program for those no longer able to be a part of the major work force. For a few, it is an interim step into a rehabilitation program or into a work situation in the community. For the majority it will continue to be their job, one in which they take great pride and find a feeling of accomplishment. The few extra dollars earned help in providing a supplement to meager monthly pension and social security checks. Many of those in our particular program have been work-oriented. They have little time or resources to pursue hobbies. This group responds much better to the work program than they do to purely social functions, craft classes, etc.

The problem of getting persons to the services and especially those individuals living in highly rural areas continues to be a problem of great magnitude. There are locations in the area in which there is no doctor within a radius of 60 miles. There are no geriatric health clinics available. Health Departments do have visiting health nurses and aftercare nurses who dispense drugs for those released from state mental institutions. The needs of the medically indigent are acute. Therefore, immediate plans call for the employment of a nurse to be a part of the Valley Program for Aging Services. She will be attached to the Health Departments in the area and will be charged with the responsibility of visiting senior centers for check-ups and referrals for other medical services. She will provide basic medical supervision for the clients of the aging program.

The information and referral component of the program involves many other community agencies. In some instances, a staffing is held with a person who has a multiplicity of problems and all agencies which could possibly be able to provide a missing piece in the network of services attends the session. In other cases, it is a matter of telephone calls, providing transportation and establishing eligibility for help. A manual referral system is used and follow-up is usually provided by center directors and/or center volunteers.

For the first two grant years, the only full-time professional positions were those of a Program Director and a work-therapy director. Part-time positions were for a secretary and a bookkeeper. Craft instructors, Work-therapy Supervisor, Drivers and Center Directors were all on an hourly or part-time basis. In the third year there are four full-time workers and ten part time workers. Monthly staff meetings are held to review and plan programs and to work out problems. Volunteer training workshops are planned by center directors, with help from community agencies and professionals (psychiatric social worker, secretary, teacher, etc.).

Over 100 students have been placed in the centers for in-service training and lab experience in the past two years. Some decide on special projects, others work with individuals and families and other agencies.

In October 1973, the Madison College Home Economics Department became the grantee for a Title VII Nutrition Project. Through this program a hot lunch is being provided once a week in each center, plus additional feeding sites. They plan to expand this service to additional days (ideally it will be increased to five days per week). A project funding by a grant under Title I of the High Education Act has also benefited the various center programs by teaching handicrafts to older Americans. The grantee for this grant also was Madison College.

The local mental health clinics have been providing individual counseling as needed and clinic staff as well as professionals from Western State Hospital and DeJarnette Hospital have served on Advisory teams for Center staff. Plans are being developed for group therapy sessions in the centers and a regular consultation service to center personnel.

Through Operation Mainstream (CAMPS and local Employment Agencies) two seniors have been hired for work-training in center programs.

The AARP groups have provided legislative back-up by bringing the needs of the elderly to the attention of local governmental bodies. They have researched tax-relief programs, collected data to determine transportation needs and helped in providing direct services in the centers, as volunteers.

Junior Women's Clubs and Jaycees and Sororities have given direct and monetary assistance to individuals at holidays and in emergencies. One Junior Woman's Club also has developed their own "adopt-a-grandparent" concept. Each young woman adopts a Senior Citizen as a grandparent, they bake a birthday cake, bring gifts and plan a party at the center. Throughout the year, they remember "their grandparent" with cards, visits, and special treats. This is not a one-way street, in that Juniors have often become interested in skills which the Seniors teach (canning, needle work, canning and preserving, wood carving, rug making, etc.). Often times pre-schoolers attend the Senior center with "mommie." The cross section of age groups and socio-economic backgrounds makes for interesting friendships and sharing.

The newest income supplement concept is a project soon to be undertaken with Handicraft Marketing Sales, Inc. (a non-profit organization set up to handle wholesale crafts for the aging in a 5 state area). This is funded through a grant from the Rehabilitation Services Administration. This program has great potential in motivating persons to upgrade their crafts.

Consignment of crafts is sought with disaster. Local bazaars and craft fairs are excellent as far as they go, but a steady market to keep persons working and selling is certainly the ideal. We have every reason to believe Handicraft Marketing Sales can develop this concept.

I hope I have been able to give some idea of our programs in the Valley and how and why they are working. The cooperation, coordination and inspiration of many varied interests, age and professional groups and agencies contribute to the life of a successful Senior Service Center.

I am afraid that I have not conveyed the meaning which these programs have for many older persons. Therefore, I would like to use a partial quote from one of our retired volunteers which perhaps says it much better than I.

The Rewarding Experience of a Volunteer

"Shortly after retirement, I came to Augusta County, Virginia to live. After the hurly-burly of a big city, I preferred the quiet beauty of the Shenandoah Valley as a place to live. Social Security, government pension and an income from small investments provided a comfortable living, yet I felt a void and a need for creative living.

I found my spot in the program of the Waynesboro Senior Center. Several months after its' beginning, I enlisted as a volunteer.

My interest in a hobby has always been in needlework, primarily needlepoint, knitting and crochet. A busy life of business career and housekeeping limited my time for indulging in my hobby. Now that I am retired, I can pursue my hobby to my heart's content, enlarging on the scope of my endeavors from a study of advanced methods and exchange of ideas with other persons at the Waynesboro Senior Center.

Our Senior Center is a place where the elderly, perhaps seeking companionship and new friends, can come and spend a few pleasant hours with others of like bent, pursue hobbies, and exchange ideas on arts and crafts.

It is also a place which offers opportunity for income supplementation on simple assembly work under contract with business establishments, the teaching of arts and crafts in a wide range of creativity, and a place for the vocationally handicapped by reason of physical impediments in hearing, speech, sight or retardation.

To cite one rewarding experience of mine, — an elderly lady from a nursing home comes regularly. A serious impediment in hearing and speech made it necessary at first to stand by her and show her, rather than tell her, every step of the way on some simple craft. With a bright mind and dextrous fingers, she learned rapidly, yet remained passive and expressionless. After working with her for several weeks, one day while I was standing by her showing her how to make some simple craft, she reached up and put her arms around me, without a word, but with a beaming face which bespoke, "Thank you, I love you." I was touched by this spontaneous response and I felt a surge of joy myself that I could contribute something to the lonely and handicapped individual."

CHAPTER 13

NURSING HOME CARE

BASIC QUESTIONS
LICENSES AND CERTIFICATES
PHYSICAL CONSIDERATIONS SERVICES
ATTITUDES AND ATMOSPHERE

FINDING a nursing home which provides the services and atmosphere a person needs and prefers takes time and effort as well as information. When you consider that nursing home becomes a person's home and community for as long as he remains there, you realize how necessary and worthwhile the search can be.

It helps to plan ahead for the future of older members of your family as well as your own later years. Individuals who look ahead find themselves better able to locate the right nursing home care at the right price or to find suitable alternatives to nursing home care and to accept the ultimate decision.

People often face sudden emergencies or serious illness and are forced to seek the first available opening in a nursing home. In such a situation knowledge about nursing home care helps lead to a good selection.

This paper tells you about the variety of institutions called nursing homes, including those called rest homes, convalescent homes, homes for the aged, or retirement homes. It also describes the kinds of care and services found in good nursing homes and provides a checklist for your use in making comparisons.

BASIC QUESTIONS

What are the alternatives to nursing home care?

An increasing number of communities provide services such as visiting nurses, therapists, homemakers and home health aides, outpatient care and "meals on wheels" to people living at home.

Some communities also have group housing programs. Such services can delay or eliminate the need for nursing home care. Sharing a home with someone who is willing and physically able to help also can provide a good solution. The longer a person can cope with life outside an institution, the longer he or she usually retains dignity and a sense of independence. For some people, nevertheless, nothing can substitute for a good nursing home. When does a person need a nursing home?

When an older person needs help with dressing, shopping, meal preparation and personal chores and when these needs cannot be filled by his family or community services, nursing home care could be needed. When an older person needs medical attention which the family cannot afford to provide at home, or when keeping him at home may severely upset family life, nursing home care could be needed. Other personal needs may also dictate the need for nursing home care.

Talk it over among the family members, including the patient. Consult your physician. If you're faced with the question of moving someone from a hospital to a nursing home, talk to the hospital's social worker.

Always consider the patient's needs and preferences. After all, his lifestyle may be changed. Everyone, regardless of age or degree of health, has a right to influence his own fate.

Consider family needs. No one needs to feel guilty about moving a loved one into a nursing home, especially if all alternatives and consequences have been carefully weighed and if the nursing home is chosen with care.

What kinds of nursing home care are available?

Some nursing homes specialize in personal service, some in medical. Others take care of residents with all kinds of needs — from help with eating to post-hospital medical care. Since a home's name tells you little about the services offered, you should make a personal visit and talk to the administrator.

The administrator may use phrases like skilled nursing home, intermediate care facility, or extended care facility. These terms have come into use as a result of two government programs — Medicaid and Medicare — which pay bills for a majority of nursing home residents. Medicaid pays bills for some low income people, while Medicare pays bills for most people over 65. Under the Medicaid and Medicare programs, homes are classified according to the kinds of services offered.

An intermediate care facility is for people who need some nursing supervision in addition to help with eating, dressing, walking or other personal needs. Medicaid programs in some States pay for intermediate care but Medicare never does.

A skilled nursing home is staffed to make round-the-clock nursing services available to residents sick enough to require them. Medicaid programs in all States pay for skilled nursing home care, if a physician says such care is needed.

An extended care facility also provides round-the-clock nursing services and medical supervision as an extension of hospital care. Medicaid programs do not apply here. Medicare pays for up to 100 days only if patients have spent at least three days in a hospital and extended care is recommended by a physician. Medicaid can usually pick up the charges after 100 days for those who are eligible.

A nursing home may be certified in one, two, or all three categories. If you expect Medicaid to pay your bills, look for a home certified as an intermediate care facility or as a skilled nursing home. If you expect Medicare to pay, look for a home certified as an extended care facility. Many homes qualify for both Medicaid and Medicare.

Under the Medicare and Medicaid programs, the Federal Government sets standards for nursing home services as well as safety and sanitation. Each State must follow these standards when it inspects and certifies nursing homes that receive money from Medicaid and Medicare. States follow their own standards in inspecting and licensing all other nursing homes.

Even if you pay your own bills, knowing that a home meets Federal as well as State standards for services, safety and sanitation, should help you choose a nursing home. What's the first step in finding the right nursing home?

Make a list of nursing homes in your area that seem to fit the patient's preferences and needs. The more choices you have, the better your chances of making the best selection. Get the names of nursing homes from your local health department, medical society, hospital or nursing home association, senior citizens and social work groups, Social Security District office, welfare or family assistance office, physician, clergyman, relatives and friends, and the yellow pages of the phone book. No single individual or group can supply complete information about all possible homes.

Should you visit all the homes on your list?

No. You can eliminate some by making a few telephone calls to determine whether a home actually provides the kind of care that is needed and whether it participates in Medicare or Medicaid if you're depending on that kind of help.

When should you visit a home?

Preferably during late morning or midday so you can observe the noon meal being served. Plan to spend at least an hour. Some homes allow you to inspect during visiting hours. It is usually best to make an appointment to see the administrator.

LICENSES AND CERTIFICATES

Most homes display their licenses and certificates. Never accept someone's word that certificates exist. Ask to see them and take time to examine them. Be sure they are current. The more important ones include:

Nursing Home License. If the home isn't State licensed, don't use it. All States require and issue licenses.

Nursing Home Administrator License. All nursing home administrators must have State licenses, except in Arizona. If the administrator does not have a current license or is unlicensed, do not use the home.

Joint Commission on Accreditation of Hospital Certificate (JCAH). A good indication, but not a sure one, that the home does its job well. The JCAH is a nongovernment organization which inspects and evaluates hospitals and nursing homes.

PHYSICAL CONSIDERATIONS

Locations

Think of whether the patient prefers a city or a country setting.

In either case, its advantageous to be near a hospital. If the patient wants to continue using his personal doctor, the home should be near the hospital where the doctor practices. Equally important, the location should allow family and friends to visit easily, since this often affects the patient's progress.

Accident Prevention

The elimination of hazards is a matter of critical concern especially when a patient can't move about easily. Most good homes emphasize accident prevention because even minor mishaps can be disastrous for the aged. All areas should be clear of small low objects which can cause a person to trip. There should be no throw rugs or small area rugs. Chairs should be sturdy and not easily tipped. Handrails in hallways and grab bars in bathrooms increase safety while they also encourage self-help.

Fire Safety

A good nursing home must comply with Federal and/or State fire safety codes. Ask to see the report of a home's last fire safety inspection showing that it meets State or Federal codes or both. Do not use a home that has not been inspected and cleared for fire safety within the year.

Good housekeeping is important in preventing fires and avoiding tragedy if one starts. Exits and the paths to exits must be clearly marked and must not be blocked. Doors must not be locked from the inside. Stairways must be enclosed and doors to stairways must be kept closed.

A good home puts residents through frequent fire drills to acquaint them with the quickest means of leaving the building wherever they may be at the moment. A written emergency evacuation plan should be available. Adequate staff should be present to aid patients who cannot walk by themselves.

Bedrooms

Each must open onto a corridor and have a window. Preferably, a bedroom should have no more than four beds, placed so as to permit easy access. Each resident should have a drapery for privacy, and a nurse call bell and fresh drinking water within reach. Each resident should have a reading light and room enough to maneuver a wheelchair easily. And each should have his own closet and drawers for personal belongings. Ask how the home selects roommates. Putting two people together without considering their special interests or personalities can lead to conflict.

Cleanliness

Among good homes, there is some variation. Does the resident prefer super-tidiness or a lived-in look? Unpleasant odors indicate a dirty home or poor attention to the incontinent. However, you may notice a slight smell of urine, because nothing can remove it completely and good nursing homes don't mask odors with highly scented sprays.

Lobby

Often used by residents as a lounge, a lobby should contain comfortable chairs and couches, plants and flowers, and a bulletin board with notices of activities and menus. Sometimes certificates and licenses as well as examples of residents' works in arts and crafts are on display.

Hallways

These should be large enough to allow two wheelchairs to pass with ease and should have hand-grip railings on either side. Some homes brighten their corridors with colorful paint and pictures.

Dining Rooms

One of the home's most important areas, it should be attractive and inviting, with comfortable chairs and tables which can be moved around and accommodate patients in wheelchairs. If you visit during the noon meal, sample the food. Notice whether it matches the posted menu. Sometimes homes try to cut costs by substituting. Patients who need help should be receiving it.

Kitchen

Food preparation, garbage and dishwashing areas must be separated from one another. Food needing refrigeration, such as milk, cream sauces and mayonnaise, should never be left on counter tops.

Activity Rooms

Larger homes have at least one activity room; smaller homes often use the dining room for this purpose between meals. Most important, residents who are not too sick should be engaged in activities of some kind — reading, craft work or games, for example.

Special Purpose Rooms

Rooms should be set aside for physical examinations or therapy and used for those purposes.

Isolation Room

At least one bedroom and bathroom should be set aside to isolate anyone with a contagious disease.

Toilet Facilities

Toilet facilities should be designed to accommodate wheelchair patients, have a sink (with hot and cold running water), and grab bars on or near the toilet. Good homes have toilet facilities for every bedroom and place a nurse call bell near each toilet. Some nursing homes provide each bedroom with a bathtub or shower (look for grab bars and nonslip floors); others have central bathing areas to make it easier to assist patients.

Grounds

Good homes encourage patients to get our of doors. Even a city home should have a lawn or garden for the patients to get fresh air, and there should be ramps to help the handicapped get around. Many homes permit patients to tend the gardens.

SERVICES

Medical Services

Every home should have a physician available in an emergency. He may be on the staff or on call. Good homes allow patients to be treated by their private physicians as often as necessary. If the patient will depend on the home's physician, find out how often he visits and how closely he supervises.

If the home has no physician on its staff and the patient has no private physician, ask how the home will assure that the patient receives regular medical attention.

Good nursing homes require a patient to have a thorough physical examination immediately before or upon admission. The doctor and nurse should also involve the patient in making a plan for his care and treatment while in the nursing home and in revising the plan as the patient's condition changes.

The patient who is mentally alert must have the final say in any matters affecting his health. He has the right to know about the tests and medications given to him during his care.

The need for other medical services, such as dental or eye care, does not stop when a person enters a nursing home. These often become more important as he grows older. The home you choose should have some arrangements with a nearby hospital or with doctors in the community — dentists, podiatrists, optometrists and the like — to see that patients get all the medical treatment they need. Be sure to ask if these arrangements exist and their costs.

Hospitalization

A good nursing home usually has an arrangement with a

nearby hospital in case patients become acutely ill. Ask the administrator what arrangements the home has and in their absence what is done in case of emergency.

Nursing Services

The competence and attitude of the nursing staff probably affects a resident's sense of well-being more than any other service. Most extensively trained of all nurses, with a minimum of two years of special education, a registered nurse (RN) should direct nursing services in homes with patients who are ill enough to need skilled nursing care. An RN may not be on duty during all shifts, but must be responsible for the nursing staff. Licensed practical nurses (LPN), with at least one year of specialized training, should be on duty day and night.

Nurses' aides, who come into contact with patients more than any other staff members, help with bathing, eating and dressing, the use of bed pans and other personal needs. Nurses' aides should have at least two to four weeks of training, followed by periodic performance evaluation and ongoing inservice training. Ask the administrator to tell you about the training program for nurses' aides.

Physical Therapy

Full or part-time specialists should be available to help patients regain lost abilities such as walking, talking, and dressing. Therapists also help develop skills to overcome deafness and other handicaps as well as occupational and recreational skills which are personally satisfying.

Activities Program

The most successful program reduces a patient's isolation — from other patients in the home and from life outside the home. For those who can go out, activities should include trips to places such as theaters, museums and parks, and visits to the homes of friends and family. Community institutions such as libraries should bring their services to the home. People from the community should be encouraged to serve as volunteers who work or visit with the patients. Each patient should have an activities schedule geared to his interests and abilities. Group activities such as games, arts and crafts and social functions, and individual activities such as reading and letter writing should be included. Residents should be encouraged but not forced to participate.

Religious Observances

Older people often like to attend religious services and to talk to their clergymen. They should be able to do both — either in the home or at a nearby house of worship. Attending religious services, of course, should always be a matter of choice.

Social Services

Good nursing homes have social workers on their staffs or as consultants to aid patients and their families deal with various problems. For example, a social worker may be able to help new patients overcome feelings of loneliness and isolation and learn how to live in a nursing home. A social worker can also help a patient's family adjust to the nursing home situation. Residents and their families should be encouraged to call freely upon a social worker for assistance and advice.

Food

A dietician should plan balanced, varied and tasty meals, which suit all of a patient's medical and personal needs. Ask to see menus. Inquire about eating rules. Good homes serve meals at normal times, allow plenty of time for leisurely eating and provide nutritious between-meal and bedtime snacks. Be sure the attendants bring meals to bedfast patients and help feed them if necessary.

Grooming

Good homes arrange for barbers and beauticians to come in if staff members cannot serve in these ways.

ATTITUDES AND ATMOSPHERE

Warmth, friendliness and encouragement help sick people get better and well people stay well. The atmosphere in a nursing home should be cheerful. Each member of the staff, from administrator to janitor, should be pleasant and show genuine, personal interest in each of the people living in the home.

The administrator and staff should be courteousn helpful, and frank in their comments; treat patients with respect, and know most of them by name. They should often stop and chat with patients. The administrator should be available to patients and family members who want to talk about special problems, questions or complaints.

Staff members should respond quickly to patients' call for assistance and treat patients with courtesy, respect, and affection. A nursing home may meet every known standard, but if its staff treats people coldly, the patients suffer.

Unless they are too sick, patients should appear to be alert and active. Some patients may prefer to sit and observe, but if most of them are passive, it may indicate that the home has no activities program or that patients are kept on tranquilizers, or both.

Residents should be allowed to decorate their bedrooms with personal belongings and to wear their own clothing. They should be allowed to communicate freely by letter or telephone without interference or censorship by the home's staff. Those residents who wish to work for themselves in the home, by doing their own laundry or cleaning their rooms, for example, should be encouraged to do so, but no one should be forced.

Visiting hours should be generous and set for the convenience of patients and visitors, not of the nursing home.

Nursing homes, by law, may not discriminate in providing services because of race, color, or national origin. The law applies to referrals, admissions, accommodations, room assignments and transfers, policies regarding financial matters, care services, physical facilities, resident's privileges, and the assignment of medical staff and volunteers.

Ask residents their opinions of the home. Ask visitors or volunteers the same question. If you see no volunteers, ask why none work in the home. If you see no visitors, ask for the names of several patients' families. Call or write them to find out what they think of the home.

Charges

The more services you require, the more you will probably pay. Talk to the administrator about the basic monthly charge and exactly what the patient receives for it: the kind of nursing care, therapy, room, meals, and so on. Some homes make additional charges for services like laundry that other homes include in their basic rates.

Itemize the extra services and supplies which the patient will probably need. Be clear whether a charge for a special mattress, for example, is a one-time charge or a monthly rate. Find out where, if possible, you can save money. For example, patients should not be required to fill their prescriptions in the nursing home pharmacy. They should be able to buy medicines from a pharmacy of their own choice which may charge less.

Find out whether the patient is entitled to Medicaid or Medicare by calling the welfare department (for Medicaid) or your local Social Security District office (for Medicare). If a patient is eligible for Medicaid the home should bill the State directly for all charges. (In a few states, nursing homes may legally ask families to contribute to the cost of patients' care. This practice is gradually being stopped, but is still in effect in Alabama, Florida, Georgia, and Louisiana).

If the patient is not eligible for one of the government programs, check into private health insurance such as Blue Cross/Blue Shield or another major medical plan to see if it covers nursing home costs.

Compare the costs of several homes. If you look at homes before a crisis arrives, you probably will be able to find a good home at a reasonable price.

Checklist

This checklist will help you compare one nursing home with

another. As a rule of thumb, the best home is the one for which you check the most "yes" answers. However, remember that different kinds of homes offer different types of services. You should compare skilled nursing homes with skilled nursing homes and residential homes with residential homes.

If the answer to any of the first four questions is "no," do not use the home.

		YES	NO
1.	Does the home have a current license from the State?	____	____
2.	Does the administrator have a current license from the State?	____	____
3.	If you need and are eligible for financial assistance, is the home certified to participate in Government or other programs that provide it?	____	____
4.	Does the home provide special services such as a specific diet or therapy which the patient needs?	____	____
5.	Location		
	a. Pleasing to the patient?	____	____
	b. Convenient for patient's personal doctor?	____	____
	c. Convenient for frequent visits?	____	____
	d. Near a hospital?	____	____
6.	Accident Prevention		
	a. Well-lighted inside?	____	____
	b. Free of hazards underfoot?	____	____
	c. Chairs sturdy and not easily tipped?	____	____
	d. Warning signs posted around freshly waxed floors?	____	____
	e. Handrails in hallways and grab bars in bathroom?	____	____
7.	Fire Safety		
	a. Meets Federal and/or State codes?	____	____
	b. Exits clearly marked and unobstructed?	____	____
	c. Written emergency evacuation plan?	____	____

d. Frequent fire drills? ___ ___
e. Exit doors not locked on the inside? ___ ___
f. Stairways enclosed and doors to stairways kept closed. ___ ___

8. Bedrooms

a. Open onto hall? ___ ___
b. Window? ___ ___
c. No more than four beds per room? ___ ___
d. Easy access to each bed? ___ ___
e. Drapery for each bed? ___ ___
f. Nurse call bell by each bed? ___ ___
g. Fresh drinking water at each bed? ___ ___
h. At least one comfortable chair per patient? ___ ___
i. Reading lights? ___ ___
j. Clothes closet and drawers? ___ ___
k. Room for a wheelchair to maneuver? ___ ___
l. Care used in selecting roommates? ___ ___

9. Cleanliness

a. Generally clean, even though it may have a lived-in look? ___ ___
b. Free of unpleasant odors? ___ ___
c. Incontinent patients given prompt attention? ___ ___

10. Lobby
a. Is the atmosphere welcoming? ___ ___
b. If also a lounge, is it being used by residents? ___ ___
c. Furniture attractive and comfortable? ___ ___
d. Plants and flowers? ___ ___
e. Certificates and licenses on display? ___ ___

11. Hallways

a. Large enough for two wheelchairs to pass with ease? ___ ___
b. Hand-grip railings on the sides? ___ ___

12. Dining Room

a. Attractive and inviting? ___ ___
b. Comfortable chairs and tables? ___ ___
c. Easy to move around in? ___ ___
d. Tables convenient for those in wheelchairs? ___ ___
e. Food tasty and attractively served? ___ ___

    f. Meals match posted menu?   ____ ____

    g. Those needing help receiving it?   ____ ____

13. **Kitchen**

    a. Food preparation, dishwashing and garbage areas
       separated?   ____ ____

    b. Food needing refrigeration not standing on counters?   ____ ____

    c. Kitchen help observe sanitation rules?   ____ ____

14. **Activity Room**

    a. Rooms available for patients' activities?   ____ ____

    b. Equipment (such as games, easels, yarn, kiln, etc.)
       available)   ____ ____

    c. Residents using equipment?   ____ ____

15. **Special Purpose Rooms**

    a. Rooms set aside for physical examination or therapy?   ____ ____

    b. Rooms being used for stated purpose?   ____ ____

16. **Isolation Room**

    a. At least one bed and bathroom for patients
       with contagious illness?   ____ ____

17. **Toilet Facilities**

    a. Convenient to bedrooms?   ____ ____

    b. Easy for a wheelchair patient to use?   ____ ____

    c. Sink?   ____ ____

    d. Nurse call bell?   ____ ____

    e. Hand grips on or near toilets?   ____ ____

    f. Bathtubs and showers with nonslip surfaces?   ____ ____

18. **Grounds**

    a. Residents can get fresh air?   ____ ____

    b. Ramps to help handicapped?   ____ ____

19. **Medical**

    a. Physician available in emergency?   ____ ____

    b. Private physician allowed?   ____ ____

c. Regular medical attention assured? —— ——
d. Thorough physical immediately before or upon admission? —— ——
e. Medical records and plan of care kept? —— ——
f. Patient involved in plans for treatment? —— ——
g. Other medical services (dentists, optometrists, etc.) —— ——
h. Freedom to purchase medicines outside home? —— ——

20. Hospitalization

a. Arrangement with nearby hospital for transfer when necessary? —— ——

21. Nursing Services

a. RN responsible for nursing staff in a skilled nursing home? —— ——
b. LPN on duty day and night in a skilled nursing home? —— ——
c. Trained nurses' aides and orderlies on duty in homes providing some nursing care? —— ——

22. Physical Therapy

a. Specialists in various therapies available when needed? —— ——

23. Activities Program

a. Individual patient preferences observed? —— ——
b. Group and individual activities? —— ——
c. Residents encouraged but not forced to participate? —— ——
d. Outside trips for those who can go? —— ——
e. Volunteers from the community work with patients? —— ——

24. Religious Observances

a. Arrangements made for patient to worship as he pleases? —— ——
b. Religious observances a matter of choice? —— ——

25. Social Services

a. Social worker available to help residents and families? —— ——

26. Food

a. Dietitian plans menus for patients on special diets? —— ——

     b. Variety from meal to meal?   ____ ___

     c. Meals served at normal times?   ____ ___

     d. Plenty of time for each meal?   ____ ___

     e. Snacks?   ____ ___

     f. Food delivered to patients' room?   ____ ___

     g. Help with eating given when needed?   ____ ___

27.   Grooming

     a. Barbers and beauticians available for men and women?   ____ ___

ATTITUDE AND ATMOSPHERE

28.   General atmosphere warm, pleasant and cheerful?   ____ ___

29.   Staff members show interest in and affection for individual patients? Are courteous and respectful? Stop to chat with patients?   ____ ___

30.   Administrator courteous and helpful?   ____ . ___

     a. Knows patient by name?   ____ ___

     b. Available to answer questions, hear complaints or discuss problems?   ____ ___

31.   Staff members respond quickly to patient calls for assistance?   ____ ___

32.   Residents appear alert?   ____ ___

     a. Residents are active and involved unless they are very sick?   ____ ___

     b. Can decorate their own bedrooms?   ____ ___

     c. Can wear their own clothes?   ____ ___

     d. Have a chance for self-expression?   ____ ___

     e. Can communicate freely without censorship?   ____ ___

     f. Can work for themselves if they wish?   ____ ___

33.   Visiting hours set for convenience of residents and visitors?   ____ ___

34.   Civil rights regulations observed?   ____ ___

35.   Visitors and volunteers pleased with home?   ____ ___

LOCATIONS OF REGIONAL OFFICES OF THE ADMINISTRATION ON AGING

REGION I

(Conn., Maine, Mass, N.H., R.I., Vt.)
J. F. Kennedy Federal Bldg.
Government Center
Boston, Mass 02203
Tel. (617)223-6885

REGION II

(N.J., N.Y., Puerto Rico, Virgin Islands)
26 Federal Plaza, AoA
New York, N.Y. 10007
Tel. (212)264-4592

REGION III

(Del., D.C., Md., Pa., Val, W. Va.)
P. O. Box 13716, Fifth Floor
36th and Market Streets
Philadelphia, Pennsylvania 19101
Tel. (215)597-6891

REGION IV

(Ala., Fla., Ga., Ky., Miss., N.C., S.C., Tenn.)
50 Seventh St. N.E. Rm. 404
Atlanta, Georgia 30323
Tel. (404)526-3482

REGION V

(Ill., Ind., Mich., Minn., Ohio, Wis.)
29th Floor
300 S. Wacker Drive
Chicago, Illinois 60606
Tel. (312)353-4695

REGION VI

(Arl, La., N.Mex., Okla., Tex.)
1114 Commerce Street
Dallas, Texas 75202
Tel. (214)749-7286

REGION VII

(Iowa, Kans., Mo., Nebr.)
601 East 12th Street
Kansas City, Mo. 64106

REGION VIII

(Colo., Mont., N.Dak., S.Dak., Utah, Wyo.)
19th and Stout Streets, Rm. 9017
Federal Office Building
Denver, Colorado 80202

REGION IX

(Ariz., Calif., Hawaii, Nev., Samoa, Guam, T.T.)
50 Fulton Street, Room 406
Federal Office Building
San Francisco, California 94102

REGION X

(Alaska, Idaho, Oregon, Washington)
1319 2nd Avenue, Mezzanine Floor
Arcade Building
Seattle, Washington 98101
Tel. (206)442-0528 (Idaho, Oregon)
Tel. (207)442-0509 (Alaska, Washington)

ADDRESSES OF STATE AGENCIES ON AGING

ALABAMA:

Commission on Aging
740 Madison Avenue
Montgomery, Alabama 36104
Tel. (205)269-6387

ALASKA:

Office of Aging
Department of Health and Social Ser-
vices
Pouch H
Juneau, Alaska 99801
Tel. (907)586-6153

AMERICAN SAMOA:

Gov. for Aging Services
Office of the Governon
Pago Pago, Samoa 96920

ARIZONA:

Division for Aging
Department of Economic Security
2721 North Central Suite 800
Phoenix, Arizona 85004
Tel. (602)217-4446

ARKANSAS:

Office on Aging
4313 West Markham
Hendrix Hall, P. O. Box 2179
Little Rock, Arkansas 72203
Tel. (501)371-2441

CALIFORNIA:

Commission on Aging
926 J. Street, Suite 701
Sacramento, California 95814
Tel. (910)445-8822

COLORADO:

Division of Services for the Aging
Dept. of Social Services
1575 Sherman Street
Denver, Colorado 80203
Tel. (303)892-2651

CONNECTICUT:

Department on Aging
90 Washington St., Rm. 312
Hartford, Connecticut 06115
Tel. (203)566-2480

DELAWARE:

Division of Aging
Department of Health and Social Ser-
vices
2407 Lancaster Avenue
Wilmington, Delaware 19805
Tel. (302)656-6836

DISTRICT OF COLUMBIA:

Office of Services to the Aged
Department of Human Resources
1329 E. St., N.W. Munsey Bldg.
Washington, D. C. 20001
Tel. (202)638-2497

FLORIDA:

Division on Aging
Department of Health and Rehabilitation Services
1323 Winewood Blvd.
Tallahassee, Florida 32301
Tel. (904)488-7798

GEORGIA:

Office of Aging, Suite 301
Department of Human Resources
1372 Peachtree Street, N.E.
Atlanta, Georgia 30309
Tel. (404)892-1243

GUAM:

Office of Aging
Social Services Administration
Government of Guam
P. O. Box 2816
Agana, Guam 96910

HAWAII:

Commission on Aging
250 S. King St., Rm. 601
Honolulu, Hawaii 96813
Tel. (808)548-3846

IDAHO:

Office on Aging
Capitol Annex No. 7
509 N. 5th St., Room 100
Boise, Idaho 83707
Tel. (208)384-3375

ILLINOIS:

Office of Services for Aging
Department of Public Aid
State Office Building
618 E. Washington Street
Springfield, Illinois 62706
Tel. (217)525-5773

INDIANA:

Commission on the Aging and the Aged
Graphic Arts Bldg.
215 North Senate Ave.
Indianapolis, Indiana 46202
Tel. (317)633-5948

IOWA:

Commission on the Aging
415 West 10th
Jewett Building
Des Moines, Iowa 50319
Tel. (515)281-5187

KANSAS

Services for the Aging Sect.
Division of Social Services
Soc. & Rehab. Services Dept.
State Office Building
Topeka, Kansas 66612
Tel. (913)296-3465

KENTUCKY:

Commission on Aging
218 Steele Street
Frankfort, Kentucky 40601
Tel. (502)564-4238

LOUISIANA:

Commission on Aging
P. O. Box 44282
Capitol Station
Baton Rouge, Louisiana 70804
Tel. (504)389-6713

MAINE:

Services for Aging
Community Services Unit
Department of Health & Welfare
State House
Augusta, Maine 04330
Tel. (207)622-6171

MARYLAND:

Commission on Aging
State Office Building
1100 North Eutaw Street
Baltimore, Maryland 21201
Tel. (301)383-2100

MASSACHUSETTS:

Executive Office of Elder Affairs
State Office Building
18 Tremont Street
Bsoton, Massachusetts 02109
Tel. (617)727-7751

MICHIGAN — Title III:

Commission on Aging
Dept. of Social Services
Commerce Center Building
300 South Capitol Avenue
Lansing, Michigan 48926
Tel. (517)373-0590

MICHIGAN — Title VII:

Dept. of Social Services
Commerce Center Building
300 South Capitol Avenue
Lansing, Michigan 48926
Tel. (517)373-0590

MINNESOTA:

Governor's Citizens Council on Aging
277 West University Ave.
St. Paul, Minnesota 55103

MISSISSIPPI:

Council on Aging
P. O. Box 5136
Fondren Station
2906 N. State Street
Jackson, Mississippi 39216
Tel. (601)982-6436

MISSOURI:

Office of Aging
Department of Community Affairs
505 Missouri Blvd.
Jefferson City, Missouri 65101
Tel. (31)751-4114

MONTANA:

Commission on Aging
Penkay Eagles Manor
715 Fee Street
Helena, Montana 59601
Tel. (406)471-2307

NEBRASKA:

Commission on Aging
State House Station 94784
Lincoln, Nebraska 68509
Tel. (402)471-2307

NEVADA:

Division for Aging Services
Dept. of Human Resources
308 North Curry St.
Carson City, Nevada 89701
Tel. (702)882-7855

NEW HAMPSHIRE:

Council on Aging
P. O. Box 786
71 South Main Street
Concord, New Hampshire 03301
Tel. (603)271-2751

NEW JERSEY:

Division on Aging
Department of Community Affairs
P. O. Box 2768
363 West State Street
Trenton, New Jersey 08615
Tel. (609)292-3765

NEW MEXICO:

State Commission on Aging
408 Galisteo Street
Villagra Bldg.
Sante Fe, New Mexico 87501
Tel. (505)827-5258

NEW YORK:

Office for the Aging
N. Y. State Exec. Dept.
855 Central Avenue
Albany, New York 12206
Tel. (518)457-7321

NEW YORK STATE:

Office for the Aging
2 World Trade Center 5036
New York, N. Y. 10047
Tel. (212)488-6405

NORTH CAROLINA:

Governor's Coordinating Council on
 Aging
Administration Bldg.
213 Hillsborough
Raleigh, North Carolina 27603
Tel. (919)829-3983

NORTH DAKOTA:

Aging Services
Social Services Board
Randal Professional Bldg.
Rural Route #1
Bismarch, North Dakota 58501
Tel. (701)224-2304

OHIO:

Division of Administration on Aging
Department of Mental Health and
 Mental Retardation
34 North High Street, 3rd Floor
Columbus, Ohio 43215
Tel. (614)469-2460

OKLAHOMA:

Special Unit on Aging
Dept. of Institutions, Social, and
 Rehabilitation Services
Box 25352 Capitol Station
Sequoyah Memorial Bldg.
Oklahoma City, Oklahoma 73125
Tel. (405)521-2281

OREGON:

State Program on Aging
315 Public Service Bldg.
Salem, Oregon 97310
Tel. (503)378-4728

PENNSYLVANIA:

Bureau for the Aging
Office of Adult Programs
Dept. of Public Welfare
Capital Associates Building
7th and Forester Streets
Harrisburg, Pennsylvania 17120
Tel. (717)787-5350

PUERTO RICO:

Gericulture Commission
Dept. of Social Services
Apartado 11697
Santurce, Puerto Rico 00910
Tel. (809)725-8015

RHODE ISLAND:

Division of Services for the Aging
Dept. of Community Affairs
150 Washington St.
Providence, Rhode Island 02903
Tel. (401)528-1000

SOUTH CAROLINA

Commission on Aging
2414 Bull Street
Columbia, South Carolina 29201
Tel. (803)758-2576

SOUTH DAKOTA:

Programs on Aging
State Dept. of Health
State Office Building #2
Pierre, South Dakota 47501
Tel. (605)224-3671

TENNESSEE:

Commission on Aging
Capitol Towers
510 Gay Street
Nashville, Tennessee 37219
Tel. (615)741-2056

TEXAS:

Governor's Committee on Aging
P. O. 12786 Capitol Station
Austin, Texas 78711
Tel. (512)475-2717

TRUST TERR. OF THE PACIFIC:

Office of Aging
Community Development Div.
Gov. of the Trust Territory of the
  Pacific Islands
Saipan, Mariana Islands 96950

UTAH:

Division on Aging
345 South 5th East
Salt Lake City, Utah 841202
Tel. (801)328-5579

VERMONT:

Office on Aging
Department of Human Services
126 Main Street
Montpelier, Vermont 05602
Tel. (802)828-3471

VIRGINIA:

Gerontology Planning Section
Division of State Planning and Community Affairs
9 North 12th Street
Richmond, Virginia 23219

VIRGIN ISLANDS:

Commission on Aging
P. O. Box 539 Charlotte Amalie
St. Thomas, Virgin Islands 00801
Tel. (809)774-5884

WASHINGTON:

Office on Aging
Dept. of Social and Health Services
P. O. 1788
410 W. Fifth
Olympia, Washington 98504
Tel. (206)753-2502

WEST VIRGINIA:

Commission on Aging
State Capitol — Rm. 420-26
1800 Washington St., East
Charleston, West Virginia 25305
Tel. (304)348-3317

WISCONSIN:

Division on Aging
Department of Health and Social Ser-
  vices
State Office Building, Rm. 690
1 West Wilson Street
Madison, Wisconsin 53702
Tel. (608)266-2536

WYOMING:

Adult Services
Department of Health and Social Ser-
    vices
Division of Public Assistance and
    Social Services
State Office Building
Cheyenne, Wyoming 82001
Tel. (307)777-7561

INDEX